THE SEVEN SECRETS OF PSYCHOTHERAPY

First Edition.

Heard and Written Down by Andrew R. Schoenfeld, Circa 2024

1st edition 2024

Dedicated to Jane, my wife.

DISCLAIMER:

The information presented is the author's opinion and does not constitute any health or medical advice. The content of this book is for informational purposes only and is not intended to diagnose, treat, cure, or prevent any condition or disease. Please seek advice from your healthcare provider for your personal health concerns prior to taking healthcare advice from this book.

Q: Why do we laugh?

A: Because we become aware of an incongruity or discrepancy.

Conclusion: The universe has a very big sense of humor.

Summary: When we fully know this, we will even laugh at the cycles of birth and death.

TABLE OF CONTENTS

INTRODUCTION: THE LIE OF LIES

We have been lied to. We have, without question, accepted falsehoods as truth. As a result, we have taught these lies to generations. It is not our fault, for we never realized what we were teaching was a lie in the first place.

The opposite of a lie is truth; the opposite of truth is delusion. When delusion, confused as truth, is fed to the masses, chaos ensues. In time, chaos becomes so widespread it is not recognized as chaos. It is accepted as reality.

Our shared reality can be experienced as a world colored with tapestries of animals, trees, plants, insects, and sky. This is called the natural world, mother nature, or our home, Earth. This is a reality where people fall in love, where children are born into their mother's arms, and where families live and grow as they celebrate seasons passing. But something has happened to the world. Its seas have become polluted, its land has become scorched, and its sky muddied. This is a reality of chaos, a reality that sadly leads people into self-loathing, emotional suffering, fear, suspicion, mistrust of others, and greed. The same chaos that scorches the land and pollutes the waters is the same chaos that leads to people disparaging themselves and others, civil, and global division, and physical conflict. This is all due to our acceptance of delusions, false beliefs of self, others and the world. We can call them delusions or lies; either way, they paint an incorrect view of life.

It might appear, due to our deluded beliefs about ourselves, that we are at odds with ourselves. We put ourselves down when we say things like "I am not good enough" or "I hate myself." On the surface, it might seem that we are at odds with others. We place ourselves above them, calling them names and wishing them harm. Similarly, when whole societies begin fighting against one another, it seems like they are at war with each other. Only on the surface is this true. Underneath the surface is the hidden, inner reality which our shared delusion will not allow us to see. Within this inner spiritual reality lives a wisdom that realizes humanity is not only at war with itself, but that it is also at war with life and the source from which it springs.

On the surface, the effects of chaos will appear to us as all the unnecessary byproducts of self, societal, and global division. That is on the surface. Here, the term "surface" applies to our physical understanding and experience of life. But underneath the facade of physical reality is an inner reality whose laws of cause-and-effect escape our awareness. We do not perceive this realm due to our deluded belief that reality is of only a physical nature. So, on the surface, we believe that our suffering is caused exclusively by the events of the physical world. One man is in a rage because another man stole from him, while another man is in the grip of grief because he lost all of his money. Now while this is only a surface understanding of things, it does not imply that these personal experiences mentioned are fictional or not registered as real. Someone hitting us or insulting us will naturally cause anything from mild upset to personal trauma. But we must understand that underneath the surface of the physical world exists a reality that says our suffering is caused not only by the effects of the physical world, but also by the chains of cause-and-effects that reside in a reality hidden to our physical senses.

When humanity accepts limiting ideas of self and others as truths, life does not sit by idly. It fights back in a way that goes unnoticed by our physical eyes which look upon the world. This is because both life and the source that gives rise to it will not allow us to mindlessly accept limitations without exacting an effect. This is difficult to understand and even harder to believe even, though for humanity it is a painful mass reality.

Unknowingly, humanity has swallowed a lie that makes the mindless acceptance of limiting beliefs possible. This lie is simply stated as such: "What we listen to in our head is a product of our thinking."

When a person says "I hate myself," or when they say to another person, "I hate you," they believe it to be true because it is simply the way they "think." As we will learn, this is not true; it is not simply "the way they think," but instead a far more complex matter that we have not been taught. When we rely upon this definition of "thinking", as a process that seems more mystical than logical, we become hostage to whatever we hear in our heads. We cannot rely forever upon the phrase, "I can't help it, it's just the way I think or feel." Without questioning where these supposed thoughts and feelings come from, we will continually fall into an unconditional acceptance of whatever crosses the hairpin of our awareness. In the end, this leads to an unquestionable acceptance of limiting beliefs — either our own, self-invented limiting beliefs, or those imposed on us via the authority of the powerful or influential — regarding what we hold as true of ourselves, others, and the world.

Beliefs of limitation are in direct contrast to the mandates of life, which are those of limitless potential. If life were to speak, it would say that by mindlessly accepting whatever we hear in our heads, we are accepting a distorted or delusional view of reality. This delusional reality is said to be *discrepant* from the mandates of harmony, balance, and limitless potential growth, the calling cards of life, itself.

This discrepancy is experienced as an emotional disruption designed to direct our attention to what we are mindlessly accepting about ourselves, others, and the world. We firmly believe that this discrepancy is the underlying cause of all of humanity's problems. We also believe that while experienced as a psychological phenomena the actual cause of discrepancy is spiritual in nature. It is imperative, if we are to effectively deal with the mental health crisis we are witnessing in the world, that we develop a better understanding of our spiritual nature and its influence on our biological and psychological well-being.

In the following chapters, we will come to dismantle the prevalent false beliefs we hold regarding mental and spiritual well-being as they are offered by the conventional ideas of self-help and psychotherapy. To replace those false beliefs, we will guide you to arrive at your own personal understanding of the hidden inner reality. This reality not only will know the truth of discrepancy, but it will also know how to undo discrepancy as it manifests.

We do not always have an answer for things that happen to us in the physical world. We cannot always control things to our liking. Certainly, everyone that has lived knows that life can be a harsh reality. But, we can seek out the answers that exist within an inner intuitive realm where clarity can soothe emotional disruption, and where wisdom can replace confusion.

To do this, we must realize that both the physical world and the inner, hidden world of which we speak are but two versions of an *ultimate reality* that stems from one wondrous law. While giving rise to both versions of reality, the law we speak of permeates through and dictates them. This dictation concerns how the fundamental law gives rise to this ultimate reality and how it operates or functions within it. It is from within this ultimate reality — a reality which operates outside of our awareness — that the true cause of both suffering and joy emanates.

When we replace our deluded idea that reality is only physical in nature, and instead begin to accept that it could be far greater than we have been taught, we will be able to walk through the door of our inner intuitive senses and touch upon the ultimate reality. In that reality, we are not merely single individuals who seemingly oppose one another, but rather we are one of a collective, far more than eight billion strong. Only as a single individual are you separate, vulnerable, or easily defeated. But when you realize that you are eight billion strong, there can be no room for defeat.

Go to www.andyschoenfeld.com for more (FREE) life-changing wisdom!

CHAPTER 1: WHO IN THE WORLD TAUGHT US THE LIE OF LIES?

Was it some evil person who wanted to take advantage of us? Was it some sociopath who wanted to divide us? Was it a politician, a dictator, or maybe an evil spirit? Was it an individual or a group of people who conspired against us? Who in the world would want us to experience ourselves as tiny and helpless, fragile or incompetent? We might have a better understanding of how this occurred by looking into the past and seeing what came before it.

What if once upon a time, there were a whole bunch of really wise people? Let's, just for argument's sake, say that they were so wise their contemporaries called them "enlightened." Now let's say that their wisdom was so great that other people naturally wanted to learn from them. Let's call these people disciples. So the "enlightened" sages lectured the disciples on all aspects of things. They taught them about the hidden reality called discrepancy. They taught them about the treasures of the mind and the teachings to unlock happiness. The sages knew of the ultimate reality that gives rise to life and taught their disciples how to align themselves with it, how to hear it, know it, and identify themselves with it.

These teachings were so great that in time they became famous. As the teachings became famous, so did the enlightened teachers become famous. Naturally, the disciples wanted to share the wisdom of their teacher so they began to go far and wide to teach others what they had learned. Within a thousand years, these teachings were spread far and wide throughout the entire world. Time passed and the teachings continued to spread. But then something happened, the world changed.

Over time villages disappeared and were replaced by cities. These cities were far different than the villages where the enlightened men taught. They had things called combustible engines that powered all sorts of new things called machines. With these machines, men could build bigger and bigger cities. With these machines, men could sculpt the earth and mine valuable minerals and natural resources. With their new machines, men could gather more wealth than the world had ever known. Having so many riches, these cities didn't have to spend time hunting for food like in the days of the enlightened men. In their spare time, men could read, write, create, and explore the wonders of their intellect. Some of the men became so smart that they were given a new title. Where once wise men were called sages, these men were now called scholars. They too taught, but not on hillsides. They taught, not disciples, but people called students in large buildings called universities. Some of the scholars became people called doctors. There were doctors of literature, doctors of economics, doctors of music, doctors of science, and even doctors of medicine.

Then, one day there appeared a doctor of psychiatry. This was a doctor who specialized in the ailments of the mind. Now we would think that a doctor who specialized in the ailments of the mind would have wanted to read and experience all the things the enlightened sages had to say about the wonders of the mind. If they could learn of the ways of the sages, they could help their patients come to cure their mind ailments. But the truth was that these were men of science and medicine. They lived in fancy homes and lived in cultured cities. Why would they be interested in someone who lived in a hut within a village that had no running water or sanitation? After all, did the sages study medicine? Could the sages prove that their methods were scientifically accurate? Did the sage work in a laboratory or a fancy office, or did they sit on a dirt floor with filthy feet and dirty clothes? So the new doctors of the mind, called psychiatrists, basically ignored ten thousand years of sacred teachings simply because those teachings could not be scientifically proven to be correct. Since they couldn't understand the teachings, since they didn't know how the teachings worked and they couldn't replicate the reported results of the teachings, they basically said, "Throw them out, and let's create our own models of the mind." And so psychiatrists began creating their models of the mind. They also created a new medicine where they could talk about their new mind models. The name of the new medicine was called psychoanalysis, the predecessor of modern-day psychotherapy.

Now, with every new invention, there were new truths to follow. But these were not just any type of truths; they were truths based on a new science of the mind. Over time these truths spread out into society. Then they spread to other societies until they spread throughout the whole world.

While everyone buys into these supposed truths, there is a small group of people who know that these truths are not true at all. They know that they are based on lies that we mindlessly accept. Instead of teaching you lies, this small group of people attempts to teach you truths that are based on the impartial laws that govern life, truths that allow us to activate and access aspects of mind that society tells you are imaginary. These are the ancient ways of masters long forgotten, ways that allow access to the boundless joy that sits within humanity.

Why are these truths secret? Maybe because in the process of creating modern-day therapy, the so-called experts tossed out ancient concepts of the attainment of happiness and replaced them with an intellectual understanding of unhappiness. Could this be because the founders of modern-day psychotherapy had no idea what the mind was capable of? Could it be that due to societal pressures, they too were caught in the web of their misconceptions? Or could it be that the sages lived in a world of dirt and filth and had practices that were in no way compatible with the sophistication of modern-day science?

For whatever reason, the modern experts taught us, and we accepted hook, line, and sinker, simple ideas that were based on delusions. After time, these delusions became the cultural norms we use to understand our moment-to-moment personal reality. They have taught us how to see ourselves and others. They have given us explanations for our emotional experiences and the reason for them. Delusions are false views of self and others. When we use delusions as the way to understand ourselves, the conclusions we come to are nothing but delusional. We might be asleep within our delusions, but life takes notice and uses its tool of discrepancy to help us correct our errors.

What if we were to get a glimpse of another version of reality? What if we could learn some of the secrets taught by those sages of long ago? They are only secret because we have invested our time in finding out what is wrong with people to find a cure for their suffering. Did anybody ever question why a fever comes upon a man? Is the fever to punish or is it to restore balance to his body, or is it both at the same time? As with suffering, did anyone bother to question if suffering is not simply an indicator that something is wrong with us, but also could be an indicator of something right within us? Who was it that came up with the concept of the oneness of suffering and happiness? It could be one of those sages who lived thousands of years ago. Why is it that we don't pay attention to what they said? It could be because we threw all those teachings out so we could come up with our own version of mental health in the form of psychotherapy.

There are rules to everything, even being crazy. Unfortunately, these are the rules we've perfected. But to tell you the truth, everyone is so invested in the self that is crazy that the rules to being sane have become a secret.

Go to www.andyschoenfeld.com for more (FREE) life-changing wisdom!

CHAPTER 2: THE GREATEST LIE EVER TOLD

There are lies, plenty of them. But there is one lie upon which everything rests, the greatest lie ever told. We were all taught this lie at a young age. Our mother was the first to ask, "What's wrong with you? All you do is think of everything that can go wrong." Our natural reply was to say, "But I'm scared nobody likes me." Having learned her lesson on mental health from the back of Reader's Digest, she would say, "Don't be crazy, there's nothing to be scared of." She was the first to tell us, "It's all in our head." We then took this lesson and used it during puberty. We would complain, "Why can't I belong to the group of popular kids?" Then we would answer ourselves with certainty. "What are you, crazy? Who in the world would want to be your friend?" Well, we got the crazy part correct, but we forgot to say, "But it's all in my head."

We entered adulthood having perfected our lack of confidence and self-deprecating manner. Just like an actor who has memorized his lines, we knew the script by heart. When our so-called friends got tired of hearing us complain about never getting the right job, or the right car, or the right date, we brought our production to a therapist. After a while, we began to trust them. We would recite our lines over and over. The therapist, never seeming to tire of listening to countless reruns of the same show, would sit and listen to our every word.

Client: I don't know why I always make the same mistake. I should have known better.

Therapist: You self-sabotage every time. I'm sorry to say, you are your own worst enemy.

Client: I just can't help it, I feel so helpless and alone. Nothing besides finding a partner interests me. I sleep a lot and…

Therapist: I know, you just can't seem to get out of your own way. But that's what happens when we're depressed.

Without realizing it, we have been fed a lie. We are told that our thoughts are indicators of some dysfunction or deficit. We are told that it is all our fault. And there it is, the greatest lie ever told. First told to us by our mother, rehearsed during our adolescence, and confirmed in adulthood by a mental health professional. You see, the lie is so deceptive that even though we see it right here in print, we still don't know what the lie is. It is so ingrained in our mindset that we mindlessly confuse it as an aspect of reality. So let's spell it out letter by letter so we can know what the greatest lie ever told is.

"What we hear in our heads are thoughts that we intentionally think." The first lie taught to us was "What we hear in our heads is a product of our thinking." The greatest lie goes further and tells us that our so-called thinking is intentional. If we have self-loathing thoughts, we are the ones intentionally doing it. If we think that we are inferior or superior to others, once again we are the ones intentionally doing it.

Do you realize the implications here? Our mother and our therapist both confirmed that there was something wrong with us. Our mother came right out and called us crazy. The therapist was a little nicer by saying we are depressed. Both of them told us that there was something wrong with the way we think. Both concluded that our faulty thinking is evidence of an underlying problem. Our mother might have told us that we need to learn how to "think positively." Our therapist might have told us that we need to learn to love ourselves. But how can we think positively when we are preoccupied by all our negative thoughts? And how do we learn to love ourselves when we hate ourselves? How in the world do we learn to love ourselves when we are told that we are our own worst enemy? Does it mean that we need to learn to love the enemy that is always in our way, or always sabotaging us?

Let's say that we're sitting in our car going through the laundry list of everything that is wrong with our lives. After listening to the voice in our head for a solid hour, we tell it to shut the hell up. This momentary attempt at clarity is then followed by another hour of "what the hell is wrong with me." The mere idea that we are doing it to ourselves scares the crap out of us. The reality that we can't get it to stop scares so much crap out of us that we don't have to take a shit for a year. Without understanding the truth, we naturally are terrified of whatever is wrong with us. Without understanding the truth, we are consumed by the tiny "I," "me," or "my" that runs around in our heads.

"I'm a mess." "Nobody ever helps me." "My life sucks." You see, the greatest lie ever told makes us small and a victim to ourselves. It debases us, calls us names, and leads us to feel alone. In the small world of I, me, or my, we are fragile and susceptible to others who we assume will either take advantage of us, put us down, or hurt us.

Within the lie, we only see others as we experience ourselves. If we continue to live our lives listening to the enemy inside of us, how can we not expect there to be an enemy around us? The lies spread like a woman's perfume; we cannot help but be covered by them. How we see ourselves, and how we think about ourselves, is the same way we see and think of others. If we are immersed in lies, then there is no way we can look upon a world of hope.

Go to www.andyschoenfeld.com for more (FREE) life-changing wisdom!

CHAPTER 3: SPARK, FIRE, BLAZE

Why do we bother to listen to a voice that puts us down, insults us, calls us names, and paints a constant picture of disaster? Why do we accept without any doubt, the words, feelings, and conclusions we come to when we are immersed in the dialogue within our head? Did we ever even ask the question as to why we accept words that hurt, words, blame, and describe us as something we would never intentionally ascribe to being? Without understanding the truth we will never be able to see the truth about us and all the others that live in the world.

Without knowledge, we are left to our fundamental impulses, which at times can get quite out of hand. We have the basic urge to complain. In the vernacular, that means getting things off our chest. Unfortunately, our current world of psychotherapy not only gives us permission, but encourages us to "vent". In the end, we spend so much time "venting" we don't ever get to ask what is the fundamental source of our complaint.

Give a person the chance to complain. Encourage them to really get into it. Allow them to offload their darkest secrets and their darkest impulses. Tell them that in the end, it will be good for them. After all, there is a wellspring of material already brewing inside of them. Hour after hour they have that voice in their head pushing them around putting them down, telling them that they are worthless. So instead of doing this alone, why not do it in the company of a stranger? Not a complete stranger, but what we can call a "friendly stranger." Someone who will listen to whatever noise is brewing in our head. Someone who will listen to all the conclusions we come to about ourselves. Someone who won't judge but be a friendly witness to the massacre that blazes right inside our heads.

The story comes full circle, almost. Someone invents the idea of psychotherapy. They tell us that our thoughts are indicators of dysfunction and a spark is created. Then they tell us that the dysfunction has its roots in our past, and now the spark becomes a flame. They invite us to tell them of all the bad things that have ever happened to us. We take their advice and become an expert at heaving up the past and swimming in the dark contents of our personal emotional history. We then become narcissistically preoccupied with our emotions, our past, and our pain. We are permitted to pull the ripcord and let that one little voice that we hear in our head scream its guts out. And now the flame turns into a blaze. We are given the impression that the forest fire of pain, if somehow vented, and released, will somehow burn itself out. We are given the consent of the friendly stranger that all of this is welcome and that they are proud of us for doing such a good job. So it's easy for us to then conclude that our emotions are special and that we have special permission to feel them.

We become sensitive to how others have hurt us. We become sensitive to how people still hurt us. We become sensitive to what others have said, still say, have done, and still do to make us feel bad. Isn't that the root of that horrible voice that rattles through our heads? Isn't that one of the roots of all bad emotions we feel? First, we were a victim of the voice in our head. Then we learn that it's there because we were (and continue to be) victimized by people who are not sensitive to our needs.

Replicate this lesson for the millions and millions of people who also have that nasty voice in their heads. Teach it to the masses until we have a whole society that is obsessed with their emotions, obsessed with what others are doing to them, obsessed with what others are saying to them. Then permit people to vent all these frustrations on the wonderful medium of social media. The spark became a flame. The flame became a fire. The fire raged until it became a blaze that burned our whole house down.

This narrative plays into our lowest impulses. We are so busy paying attention to all the people that do us wrong, that we have forgotten that it all started with a voice in our head. A voice that we have been permitted to purge, regurgitate, and vomit not only on the friendly stranger but on all the other mean strangers that live in the world. Other people have to tolerate our sensitivities all because we are victimized by a single voice we hear in our head. Other people have to put up with our whining and complaining, our bitching and moaning all because we can't deal with the voice that screams in our heads. The idea that we are special and no one can take our feelings away from us is a nice idea, but it does not address the two things we started with. A voice in our head that does not shut up and the most often quoted sentence in a society of sleeping people. "I can't help it, it's just the way I feel".

We have been taught to purge what is wrong to find out what is right. We have been taught that our pain stems from the past. We are taught that happiness is the absence of suffering so we have become experts in dissecting pain. We have gotten to the point where happiness cannot be found unless we dive into and swim within, and vomit the contents of our misery onto the lap of the friendly stranger. We have come to expect that the world should have the sensitivities of our friendly strangers. This is not fiction, this is the world that we live in. The trouble is that we are so busy with our self-absorbed preoccupations that we do not realize that every house in the world is burning down.

CHAPTER 4: THE TRUTH THAT UNDOES THE GREATEST LIE EVER TOLD

We are told that what we hear in our heads are our thoughts. We're also told that if it is taking place in our head, then we are the ones thinking it. This is not true; what we hear in our head is not intentionally or consciously-driven; it is driven by our subconscious mind. It is not our fault for having delusions; false views of self and the world. This should be a game-changer for us. It should also be a game changer for our friendly strangers who work with the idea written in the first paragraph. When we spew words that put us down and limit our potential, and the friendly stranger talks back to those words, they are jointly elevating delusion to the level of conscious intent. When we are alone and respond to a voice that puts us down or limits our potential, then we are doing the same thing: we confuse subconsciously-driven delusions with conscious intent.

Without understanding that we are not consciously doing this, we — along with our friendly stranger — will conclude that there is some kind of underlying condition at the root of the suffering. After all, what kind of woman goes around saying to herself, "Irene, you stupid old cow"? We naturally conclude that she has "issues" that need to be "resolved." If we were to ask her why she calls herself such names, we would once again hear the most quoted phrase of a society that accepts delusion as reality: "I can't help it, it's just the way I feel." The greatest lie, when understood, will tell us that "we can't help it," as long as we do not realize that "we" are not intentionally doing it. The same applies to the saying, "easier said than done." If we came upon a person who was in pure panic, and we told them, "There is no reason for such worry," they would reply, "You might be right, but it's easier said than done!" When we realize that our worry is not something that we are intentionally doing, but rather is something that we mindlessly *listen* to as it wells up from our subconscious mind, then we begin to get closer to being able to do something about it.

The source of our suffering is not what has happened in the past, but actually is rooted in what we are doing mindlessly in the present moment. We cannot stop this "mind vomit" when we fall into the emotional rip-tide it creates. We cannot stop the voice from putting us down, discrediting us, or limiting our abilities if we continue to mindlessly swim in the emotions that it generates. It's like kicking our legs in the ocean as a shark appears. We have to learn to stay still, and if we are lucky enough to not be bleeding, the shark will go away.

Go to www.andyschoenfeld.com for more (FREE) life-changing wisdom!

CHAPTER 5: WELCOME TO THE MOTHER OF ALL RULES

We have been told what we hear in our head are our thoughts, and that we are the ones doing it. When someone asks us what we do in our head, we assume it is called "thinking." This is incorrect, for we are not thinking; we are mindlessly listening. We are mindlessly listening to the contents of our subconscious mind as it reacts to what is happening within and around us. This friends, is the sacred teaching called The Mother of All Rules.

Ninety-nine percent of the time, we are mindlessly listening to the contents of our subconscious. When we hear words that put us down or place us above others, we are not thinking, but rather are mindlessly listening to and accepting false views of self and others. The process works independently, just like our bowel and bladder. To undo the greatest lie ever told, we need to know that we are neither intentionally nor consciously doing it. Remember the phrases, "We are our own worst enemy," and "We are self-sabotaging and always getting in our own way"? Understand that they are completely false. We are neither consciously nor intentionally trying to "think" that way. We are *not* our worst enemy; we are our best friend. We are not self-sabotaging; we are only operating according to the hidden beliefs that we hold in our subconscious. We are not getting in our own way; we are mindlessly listening to beliefs and acting them out in daily life. There is no enemy inside of us.

We would all benefit from realizing the implications of what was just said. All these years, we mindlessly assumed that our "thoughts" were indicators of our emotional unbalance. Try to imagine all the thousands of hours we were consumed with a voice we mindlessly accepted as real. Take a look at all the wrong conclusions we came to regarding ourselves. We have called ourselves losers, not good enough, and stupid. We concluded, based on what we mindlessly listened to in our heads, that there is something fundamentally wrong within us. And then, there are our friendly strangers. They might have gotten a little closer by telling us our thoughts are an indicator of an underlying problem, but they were not talking about the underlying hidden reality of which we have been speaking. The underlying problems they were looking for are found in the countless, painful experiences of our past. Remember, our friendly stranger's mind model is based on the idea that happiness is the absence of suffering. As a result of this logic, we have become experts in dissecting pain. Remember all those friendly stranger sessions where they told us to go back to those painful memories? Remember them encouraging us to vent, "get it off our chest," to stop repressing our tender emotions? Remember blaming our parents, our siblings, the other kids in school, or our teachers? It may have been a cathartic release, but in the end, we could ask if it was all necessary.

Imagine if you were a friendly stranger reading this for the first time. You would naturally begin to question a few things. You would come to realize that all of your client's complaints were unconsciously spewed onto your lap. You would come to see that when you spoke back to their *spew* (i.e. their subconscious delusions), you were engaging in a mindless dialogue. You might be horrified that you actually encouraged the clients to cough up years of memories and for them to experience the full weight of their emotional reactions. You could also be horrified that you elevated a subconscious process up to the level of a conscious, intentional idea. You listened to delusion and talked back to it. And this didn't take place once; it took place hour after hour, day after day, and year after year — all along you listened to and responded to the client's false views of self and the world. Worse yet, you may not even have known that it was all based on delusions. You normalized the whole event based on what the client said was rumbling through their head.

Go to www.andyschoenfeld.com for more (FREE) life-changing wisdom!

CHAPTER 6: WE MISUSE LANGUAGE

We use the term "delusional" for people who are crazy and in particular those who hear voices and see things that are not there. If someone can pull that off, act normal, and tell you that they hear your Aunt Suzie in heaven, then they are called "mediums." But if they act anxious, have poor hygiene, and freak us out, then they are called "psychotic." Our friendly strangers would say that this individual suffers from a delusional disorder. This comes from a society that is the world's largest distributor of weapons systems and from a world that has rules that apply to war. To our world, a so-called "justified war" is not delusional, but is an accepted fact of life. How sick is that?

The opposite of a delusion is called "truth" or "reality." We mistakenly consider the idea that killing people is justified to be a truth. We have created an intellectual understanding of humanity enabling us to rationalize and justify our actions. We accept war as a reality and then complain that the world is in chaos. Maybe this is why we fail to see a world of possibilities and look upon a world in pain with certainty. Maybe this is because we live in a world where people hold many delusions and false beliefs about themselves and others.

Go to www.andyschoenfeld.com for more (FREE) life-changing wisdom!

CHAPTER 7: THE WONDERFUL WORLD OF DIAGNOSIS

Our moment-to-moment reality is filled with an internal dialogue that speaks on its own. It is a continuous commentary that speaks its opinions and is free of any filter. This internal voice can be brutal, harsh, and unrelenting, as it gives its analysis of what is currently happening, what could happen, and what has happened in our lives. The content of its reasoning stems from the beliefs that we hold regarding ourselves, others, and the world. What it says is not up for debate, for its reasoning is not simply an opinion, but a fact. This does not mean we always happily agree with these so-called facts. We can be terrified when we hear it tear us down, debase, or humiliate us.

Similarly, we can be rallied when we hear it blaming others or putting others down. The fact that we mindlessly accept these beliefs instead of questioning their validity is, in itself, delusional. The fact is that we only solidify our identification with the delusions when we attempt to understand ourselves or others through a voice that mindlessly speaks lies. When we hear this internal voice put us down, we conclude that we are sad. Hearing this same dialogue day after day leads us to conclude that we are depressed. Our friendly strangers would say this is called a depressive disorder. When we hear it tell us all of the scary "what-ifs" (such as, "*What if* we run out of money" or "*What if* we get sick?"), we conclude that we are anxious. Our friendly strangers would say that it is called an anxiety disorder. Instead of realizing that we are accepting delusion as a reality, we — along with our friendly strangers — identify and label ourselves based on false views or mind vomit. All variations of this type of diagnostic technique have the same internal flaw, namely that they mindlessly tie us to our delusions.

Everyone's subconscious self comes up with a diagnosis. That might sound confusing, but it is more accurate than saying everyone diagnoses themselves. That sentence is just not accurate. When we sit around listening to hours and hours of delusions — ramblings which we could rightfully call *mind vomit* — and conclude that we are depressed, or a loser, or any negative conclusion, what we are really doing is listening mindlessly to the mind vomit in our head and forming conclusions about ourselves on the basis of the vomit. This conclusion is not something that we think but is something to which we mindlessly listen. Now, who in the world would form a conclusion using mindlessly driven data? It might be commonplace for the average individual to identify themselves via their limiting beliefs, but where in the world did they learn it? Who would teach anyone to use words that hurt, distort, or humiliate to form an identification of self? Could it be something we've learned by watching TV. or something that we have read in a book? Was it something our parents or friends taught us, or could it possibly be something we have learned from the modern-day industry called psychotherapy?

Our friendly strangers listen to us as we put ourselves or others down. They use what they hear to formulate a diagnosis. In doing so, they are basing their diagnosis on mind vomit. These false ideas, views, or beliefs are not being intentionally spoken. They are driven by the subconscious mind that operates independently of our conscious intention. When our friendly strangers accept these false views as credible, they are mindlessly elevating delusion to a level of conscious intent. Remember the first friendly stranger who had thrown out all the books written by sages regarding the attainment of happiness? He was the one who started to create our current models of the mind that seek an intellectual understanding of unhappiness. Since then we have become experts on unhappiness and now somehow believe that a person can be led to the holy grail of happiness through understanding misery.

Delusions are inherently limiting beliefs. They paint an incorrect picture of life. They breed suspicion and mistrust. They cause confusion and fear. They are the opposite of the truth about life and human beings. They are lies that fester within the subconscious. When our friendly strangers identify a person with that person's delusion, they insult that individual's dignity as a creator. It is like using the worst aspects of an individual's life to define them. Such identifications do not lead people to the innate happiness they already possess. Such faulty theories give the impression that through investigation of mindlessness, people can awaken.

Before the days of antidepressants, it was not uncommon for our friendly strangers to say that our issues were our fault. That is the lie that says that we are our own worst enemy. But since the advent of antidepressants, they now have a new catchphrase that softens the blow. Instead of coming out and saying our problems are our fault, they can now say that our problems result from a chemical imbalance in our brains. Of course, it's never mentioned that their mind model investigates and glorifies human suffering as a way to alleviate it. Of course, it's never mentioned that their entire model of diagnosis is based on listening to delusion and using that delusion as a way of understanding people. Of course, it's never mentioned that our friendly strangers engage with our delusion and talk back to it, thereby elevating it to the level of conscious intent. When our friendly strangers fail in their attempt to help us, they can fall back on the idea that our problems are the result of a chemical deficiency in our brains. It's a good marketing campaign that sells billions of dollars worth of drugs, but it begs the question, "If unhappy people have a chemical imbalance, then do happy people have some kind of genetic superiority?" After all, the unhappy people's genes don't work the same as the happy people's genes, so maybe that means the unhappy ones are genetically inferior. Can we remember any time in modern history when someone claimed the genetic superiority of one race over another? How did that marketing campaign go? Equally crazy is the concept of a "social index," a device with which a government will gauge an individual's worth against their cost to society.

Do we wonder why the world is in the shape that it is in? Do we wonder why greed, the bastard child of fear, is so rampant? Should there be any question as to why the people of the world are so divided when the things we use to identify people are based on delusion, false views, and mind vomit? Such an approach to understanding the human condition naturally leads people to be terrified of themselves and terrified of the other-selves whom they see in the world. This is not the fault of a single individual or group. Mass delusion leads to mass chaos. Mindlessly accepting false views of self and others as a way to understand ourselves and others only sets the collective thermostat to a boiling temperature. We might feel horrified, but at the same time, not take it personally when we hear of children shooting other children in school. We might feel shocked when we hear of the atrocities of war, though still do not feel any sense of personal responsibility for it. As long as we use delusions, false beliefs about the self and others, or mind vomit to understand ourselves, we cannot bring down the collective temperature of the world. We must begin to question the very model that we use to understand humanity for there to be any humanity left.

Go to www.andyschoenfeld.com for more (FREE) life-changing wisdom!

CHAPTER 8: THE HYPNOTIC "CRAP" – TWO SIMPLE QUESTIONS

Why do people listen without question to a voice that puts them down, hurls insults, and debases them? To begin to get to an answer, we will ask a simple question: Why is it that we don't consider ourselves a crappy person when we crap?

We all know that there is nothing that can compare to the fresh stench of clarity. A single whiff falls from the byproducts of digestion and happily dances through the chambers of our nasal cavity. The senses recoil at the wafting intake of combustion as it jolts everyone into a mind-numbing state of awareness. As we come to a gagging reality, our hope rests in the comfort of applying the two-ply tissue that is conveniently sitting by our side. There is no sense of personal humiliation. Absent are words that hurt and humiliate. People do not define themselves by the experience, but instead, casually accept the fact that defecation is a byproduct of digestion. We all accept that it is a normal part of life. So why in the world do humans make such a big deal when crap spills in their heads? The answer is not as complex as it might seem.

When an internal voice comes from out of nowhere and begins to hurl insults at us, we become hypnotized by the ferocity of the "mental defecation." We mindlessly accept that it is "real." The process is seamless and happens beyond the speed of light. We hear words in our heads that put us down. We feel emotion, the glue of our moment-to-moment personal reality. We all mindlessly conclude that it is a product of our "thinking," and that we are the ones doing it. Buying into what we hear only increases the power of the emotion. The power of emotion only intensifies the screaming voice in our heads. The more we listen to it, the more we want it to stop. The more we cannot stop it, the more emotion is generated. The more emotion is generated, the louder and more persistent the voice gets, and this goes on and on and on. Then an educated friend tells you, "You're not thinking. You're just listening to mind vomit spilling." Naturally, anyone would reply, "This is not vomit. It is real!" Then, the friend will reply, "Yes, the emotion is real, but it is being created all on its own by your subconscious." Upon hearing this, anyone would ask, "What in the world do you mean?"

To demonstrate how the process works, we will ask the second question: what did you have for dinner last night? So I would ask you, my dear reader, to ask yourself that same question. And if you did not have dinner last night, then ask about what you ate yesterday for breakfast or lunch.

Whether for a brief moment or a few seconds, you just took your eyes off the page and started moving them around. This is what happens when you are "searching" for an answer. Now let us ask: did you see just a picture, or did you just hear a word or two? The most common answer is "I just saw a picture." Once the picture came up in your mind, you then heard your brain turn the picture into language. Your subconscious heard the question, "What did you eat for dinner yesterday?" And then, your eyes naturally began to search for the picture. You referred to this process as "thinking." But can we call it "looking for something?" And then when you heard the picture turned into words and you listened to it, did you not also call that "thinking?" Perhaps we can learn to call it "listening" instead?

People might ask, "Why is this such a big deal?" It is a big deal because it *is* a big deal. It demonstrates how our subconscious gives us information based on the questions we ask. When we ask a question, our eyes start moving around in search of an answer. Then, once the picture is spotted, our brain turns it into words. Without any awareness, we mindlessly repeat what we hear in our heads. Until we brought the answers to our awareness, they rested comfortably within the confines of our subconscious. The intent was to find an answer, but then everything else happened on its own.

Your subconscious mind and the internet have something in common: they both work to retrieve massive amounts of data within the blink of an eye. The data is already there. When you type in the information bar you ask for the data to be retrieved. But when it comes to our personal experiences, are we asking questions with conscious intent? Or is it the alternative, that we passively and mindlessly listen to programs of vast discontent? Do human beings intentionally ask how to be scared when they wake up in the middle of the night? Do they ask how to be depressed, or how to see life as one endless burden to carry? Is it our intention to feel that we don't belong, that we have no purpose, or are all those things seemingly happening on their own? Who in the world would want to be scared, depressed, or self-destructive? The answer is the person who mindlessly listens to the voice in their head, as they are completely unaware that they are listening to anything at all.

So why do we believe that which we mindlessly listen to? Why do people accept without any doubt the words, feelings, and conclusions that are byproducts of immersion within the dialogue in our heads? We all must question why we accept words that hurt, blame, and describe ourselves as anything that we would never consciously ascribe to being.

The reason why we listen can be broken down into four simple parts. First, the process is seamless, happening beyond the speed of light. Second, we hear a voice in our head and assume we are the ones thinking it. Third, we feel the emotions that go along with the words to which we are listening. Fourth, under the weight of emotion, we believe what we are listening to is true.

Go to www.andyschoenfeld.com for more (FREE) life-changing wisdom!

CHAPTER 9: EMOTION IS THE GLUE OF PERSONAL REALITY

Do you remember, when I asked you what you had for dinner yesterday, seeing a picture and then hearing words to describe the picture? Intellectually, it all makes sense, especially if it is a simple memory of what you ate. What we call "thinking" is really a process of seeing pictures and listening to the words that describe them. Intellectually, it's simple to understand. But it is not so simple to grasp when what we are seeing is loaded with emotion. If, during last night's dinner, you threw up on your girlfriend's parents, the memory would lead to feeling horror and embarrassment. If someone were to say to you, "Hey, calm down. That was yesterday! Besides, you're not thinking you're an asshole or that she will break up with you. You're only mindlessly listening to the delusional vomit in your head." You would look at them and say, "That's not vomit, it's real!" And there it is: emotion is the glue of one's personal reality. When we hear words and feel strong emotions, then we assume that what we are listening to is real. This reality quickly changes when your girlfriend calls you to apologize for serving you too much alcohol. Now, with a sense of relief, you can see how your mind "spun out of control."

But life does not always work that way. Our boss does not call up in the middle of the night to reassure us that we won't get fired. The bank doesn't send a representative to our house to say that there is always a way to work out a late mortgage payment. So, while we sit in the emotion of upset, we do not question the reality of what we listen to in our heads. This is a hypnotic reality, fueled by delusion and the emotion that it generates. The second the emotion stops, the reality of what we were listening to evaporates.

When it comes to listening to a voice that puts us down, there are many reasons why we would want that emotion to go away. It feels horrible. It easily becomes combustible. It is like wearing a wet pair of jeans on a cold day. Hearing that we are our own worst enemy does not help. To cope with an enemy that we can neither touch nor see, we naturally begin to look outside of ourselves for an enemy to blame. This human tendency to blame others for our internal dissatisfaction does not go unnoticed by those who have vast control over our societies. Those who assume power know how to manipulate the masses. They know that the fuel for delusion is fear. They know that if they turn up the volume on the 'fear dial,' then the delusional and mindlessly accepted mind vomit will not stop. When it comes to hearing a voice that puts you down, it is natural to want to know how to lessen the emotional impact. But for those in power, it is just the opposite. They know that if we are bombarded with messages of fear, the mindlessly accepted mind vomit will continue to spill. Our friendly strangers are not trying to freak us out when they say there is an inner enemy with which we must deal. They are only working within the constraints of what society has allowed them to learn. But this is not the case for the power base of this world. The powerful use fear to get us to fall into our lowest impulse, the one that blames others for our internal suffering. The indicators are readily apparent. Forty-three percent of the American public believes that we are on the verge of a civil war. Immigrants are unwanted by the majority of the countries of the world. And as borders of sovereign states are invaded by military force and slaughtering civilians in the process, other countries grow fearful of the threat of invasion. Delusion becomes truth when the delusion is repeated over and over again. It is common to hear that the problems of a given society are caused by those who, like vermin, infest and infect. The powerful sell the message that others are poison to the blood of a nation, and society accepts this message in the name of national unity. Power lies in being able to lie and have others assume it is the truth. Say it over and over, and it becomes the gospel. Turn up the emotional volume, and the mind vomit continues to flow. Continue to turn up the emotional volume, and you create a hypnotic reality that is unbreakable. Play into humanity's lowest impulse and get everyone to believe their dissatisfaction is caused by an approaching enemy. Once the emotional engine of dissatisfaction is revved up, then no matter what anyone says to the contrary, the enemy is real.

There should be no question as to why there are so many unhappy people. The world has taught us to point the finger either at ourselves or at others for the cause of our suffering. This is not due to some vast worldwide conspiracy, for the flash point of human delusion is too vast to be controlled by any one group of people. What you see in the world is the result of the chaos that delusions can sow. The power of hypnotic truth blinds people to the idea of manipulation. They do not consider themselves to be fooled. Instead, they consider themselves to be lucky enough to have someone to tell them the truth. Whoever is doing the marketing realizes that perception becomes reality when placed within the pull of strong emotions. But, is it? Under the weight of delusion, it is a distorted perception that cannot be erased. Remember the greatest lie ever told, that what we hear in our heads are our thoughts and we are the ones doing it. Take that lie and pour some emotion over it, and you have the formula to convince anyone of anything as long as you say it loud and long enough. Anyone who knows this can create an ironclad delusional perception that cannot be questioned.

Go to www.andyschoenfeld.com for more (FREE) life-changing wisdom!

CHAPTER 10: HOW DO YOU KNOW THAT IT'S DELUSION?

Under the emotional weight of delusions, facts do not matter. The only fact that is registered is the feeling of intense dissatisfaction that the "facts" create. This type of manipulation is brilliant, for it makes truth into a revolving door. It sets one person's 'facts' against another person's 'facts,' juxtaposing them to the point where no one bothers to question if their 'facts' are delusional in and of themselves. Emotion is the glue of personal reality, leading us to think that "if you feel it, then it is real." Ramp up the emotional volume, repeat the same thing over and over, and no one will bother to question if what they are hearing is false.

A man will not question a voice that tells him he is inferior. He will feel dissatisfaction, but he will not question the base assumption that he is worthless. A whole society will not question their leader's voice when they say your problems are caused by "those on the other side of the aisle" or "those invading our country." The public will feel dissatisfaction with their daily lives, yet will not question the base assumption that "others are doing it to us." The whole world is at war, as one group of people blames another for their misery. No one questions the base assumptions that lie at the root of humanity's suffering.

When you blame yourself for your emotional pains, then you solidify your identification with what you hear in your head. We listen to the delusion of inferiority and mindlessly accept it. When you blame others for your emotional pains, then you solidify your identification with what you hear in your head. We listen to the delusion that we are superior to others and we mindlessly accept it. Everyone has their version of the facts, but what is the common denominator across them all? This world says that if the voice in your head puts you down, then you have an inferiority complex. It is recommended that, if your standard version of psychotherapy does not work, then it is not your fault because of the chemical imbalance in your brain. In this same world, putting others down is an acceptable way of finding peace and security. Why is it that when an individual puts themself down and debases their potential as a human, it is seen as some kind of mental illness that is rooted in an underlying cause? Yet, why do we not call it a mental illness when people debase other members of their society or those in other societies? Does the whole world need to visit a friendly stranger? Should we start sprinkling antidepressants into the atmosphere? If we became aware of the common denominator, then maybe things could change for the better.

The common denominator is that we are all human and subject to the impartial laws that govern our human existence. When we go against these laws, there is a consequence or an effect.

A reality of being human is we are all designed to feel an emotional disruption or sense of dissatisfaction when we mindlessly and unquestioningly accept delusions as truth. This experience is the indicator that tells us that we are accepting delusion as reality. This is the experience called *discrepancy*.

One could ask, how does putting ourselves down lead to the same result of emotional dissatisfaction as when we put down others? The effect of mindlessly listening to a debasing internal voice is an immediate experience of emotional dissatisfaction. But the long-term effects of putting others down can take time to manifest. The temporary effect can actually be uplifting, providing us with feelings of power, righteousness, and personal security. But there are consequences. When fueled by emotions, we may mistakenly justify delusions of superiority. When we continue to raise the message of national, moral superiority, then we have the ingredients for a "just" war. How many more times must we listen to countries declare that "this atrocity will not go unpunished"? And where is the sanity in the phrase "a *just* war"? Many things are said and emotionally felt before anyone raises a stick, arrow, or gun. Within any society exists those who possess wisdom and judgment, and their guidance could avert things like war. But do we listen to them? No. Before a war begins, the public must be sold on the idea of war. This is not a matter of opinion. The world has been sold the necessity of spending trillions of dollars to perfect the art of killing. The joke is that we are told that we must build up our forces before the enemy builds up theirs. As a result, it provides the supposed enemy with the perfect reason to do the same. Is it not interesting that we use nuclear weapons as *deterrents* to war? Would it not be a better idea to simply stop fighting with one another? Would it be a tad wiser to realize that blowing each other up is not a good idea? Fueled by the emotions of fear, we mistakenly believe that our delusions regarding other people actually are true. Those who hold these delusions believe them to be justifiably correct. We should notice that while there is a sense of emotional relief in seeing the "enemy" slaughtered, there comes with it a long-term, spiraling effect. How does it feel to belong to the species that has killed off over a billion people in a two-thousand-year period? Do we mindlessly disdain ourselves and others simply because we are a moronically flawed species bent on intentionally killing off one another? Or, could it be possible that we are merely fooled by an emotional-fueled, hypnotic reality?

The effect of mindlessly listening to a voice that discredits us is the same as the effect of listening to a voice that discredits others. In the case of the latter, however, it takes more time for that effect to become apparent. To unravel the effects created by both situations, we must learn more about the common denominator of *discrepancy*. In the case of a single individual who mindlessly accepts the message of a depreciating voice, the result is self-loathing. In the case of a society where people mindlessly accept that they are above others, the result is civil unrest. Yet, self-loathing or hatred of others is not the only cause of our emotional suffering. That is only what sits on the surface. Underneath, as previously discussed, there exists the hidden reality that tells us that our dissatisfaction is actually a symptom of life's law of balance: discrepancy.

Go to www.andyschoenfeld.com for more (FREE) life-changing wisdom!

CHAPTER 11: THE REAL REASON WHY WE ARE EMOTIONALLY DISTURBED

We are not emotionally disturbed because there is something wrong with us. We are emotionally disturbed because something inside of us is not disturbed, and it's trying to get our attention.

The true nature of our life is the true nature of all life. This is the true nature of the ultimate law. It seeks balance and harmony. Life has sprouted within us a free will, the ability to choose. Tethered to our delusions and the emotions they create, we do not consciously choose. We mindlessly accept a voice that speaks of hate and fear. This is not a choice, but rather a forced mandate. "Natural" choice follows the mandates of *what you are*, a life that is living as a human. The natural mandate is found in the simple phrase, "Do unto others," and elucidated in the words, "Don't kill, love your neighbor, don't lie, and do not steal." These do not have to be seen as commandments but rather as words of logic and reason offered to us by life itself. Anytime a person follows a forced mandate, mindlessly driven by delusion and mindlessly accepted as reality, they are biologically designed to feel a sense of emotional disruption and internal dissatisfaction. Again, this dissatisfaction is called discrepancy. Human beings experience this disruption not because they are first, disordered, chemically unbalanced, mentally ill, or emotionally disturbed. It's really the other way around. People experience such conditions because life will not allow them to mindlessly hurt themselves or others without vying for their attention. Yes there are such things as chemical imbalances in the brain, but the imbalance is not the cause, it is an effect brought on by an internal guidance system inherent in life. Since we do not scientifically understand this guidance system we are left to say it is of a spiritual nature.

If you are having a hard time believing that there is an internal guidance system within humanity, then take a look at what is happening within your personal, familial, communal, or societal world within which you live. Delusion causes division within us and between us. Delusions are false views of self and the world. Delusion causes the divisions between ourselves and others that live in the world. The mindless acceptance of delusions leads us to a sense of emotional disruption that is working to help us restore balance within ourselves and our world. But if we do not understand how discrepancy works then delusion will only lead us to either blame ourselves or others for this dissatisfaction. If you blame yourself, then you will begin to find reasons to hate yourself. If you blame others, you will find reasons to hate them. Self-loathing leads to destructive self-behaviors, and hatred of others leads to outward destructive behavior.

We have to ask ourselves if we are satisfied with some of the things which we accept as reality. High rates of suicide, children shooting other children in schools, and social and political division are rampant. We spend trillions of dollars on weapons and encourage other nations to do the same. But do we find any true satisfaction in perfecting the "art of war" or in winning a "justified war?" Do we find true satisfaction in the form of vengeance? If anyone does, then they should seriously examine whether their concept of satisfaction is delusional. Satisfaction is not dictated; satisfaction is an outcome. It is not a commandment; it is a causal reality.

Harmony and balance allow the planet to grow. Harmony and balance allow humanity to potentialize its treasures of learning, realization, and compassion. Understanding discrepancy is the prescription for rising above the voice of a forced mandate held by the grip of delusion. It is the way to bring all forms of itself to their highest order. If we learn how to utilize discrepancy, then we can find satisfaction within ourselves and our world. If we continue to follow a forced mandate based on fear, then we will only experience its consequential effects. This medicine is at times bitter, but if we try, we can taste the sweetness in it. And while this medicine is at times harsh, we can learn to find its tender aspects. This medicine breaks our hearts open not to hurt us, but to save us. It intends not to save us from ourselves, but to save us so that humanity can reclaim what is within itself. The self we see in the mirror is only *who we are*, namely a memorized version of events. On the other hand, *'what we are'* is capable of observing realities that lie beyond the perceptions of the physical senses, realities where we can perceive discrepancy working within us. Delusion causes people to see an illusion, a false view of self. The medicine of life will save us from the illusionary reality that our delusions cause us to see. It will allow us to see within our human condition and find the sanctity of life. The medicine of life will allow us to see within others the same sanctity. This medicine will save humanity not only by breaking open its heart (if need be), but also by breaking open the heart of the entire world within which it lives.

CHAPTER 12: UNDERSTANDING DISCREPANCY, THE TRUE EFFECT OF ACCEPTING DELUSION AS REALITY

When a person mindlessly accepts a voice that puts them down, they will assume that the cause of their dissatisfaction is due to something broken within themselves. They will feel "bad" because they are not good enough to get the right job or find the right relationship. When a person mindlessly accepts a voice that puts others down, they will assume that the cause of their dissatisfaction is due to something that is broken within others. They will feel "bad" because supposedly inferior people are either taking things from them or eventually will take things from them. As previously stated, the common denominator in both situations is the emotional feeling of dissatisfaction or disruption. A volcano erupts due to pressure within the volcano, it erupts to restore balance. When a person accepts limiting beliefs that put them down or place them above others, then an imbalance is registered within that individual. This imbalance needs to be restored. The medicine that life provides is what we have called *discrepancy*.

Discrepancy, a sensation of distortion, is the energetic distance between delusion and life's internal guidance system that works within humanity. If a person mindlessly accepts a voice that puts them down or places them above others, they are working against the reality of life, the natural order of harmony and balance. The human species will not move forward as a whole if we discredit ourselves, and likewise, it will not find forward movement when we discredit others. Under the spell of personal hypnosis, a person will say that what they hear in their head and feel in their body is "real." This is only the reality that sits on the surface. Underneath, there is a hidden reality. The hidden reality in this situation is not your deluded mind vomit; the reality is life's attempt to draw your attention to your errors. Life works twenty-four hours a day, seven days a week, all in order to lift us to a more accurate understanding and experience of our own potential. Its aim is for us to identify with the vast potential that is our life. Life seeks to grow and potentialize all things towards harmony and balance. When we act against the natural mandates of life, life will naturally work to correct us. The experience of emotional disruption is unsettling. One might ask about this: "If life is 'good,' why would it provide us with an experience of intense dissatisfaction?" The answer is "Because life is good it won't let us crap all over ourselves and others without trying to help us clean things up". When we mindlessly put ourselves or others down, we fall under the impression that what we are hearing in our heads is the truth. A person can go their whole life living with this distorted truth and the dissatisfaction that comes along with it, or they can arrive at the tipping point where they must find another alternative by which to live. The thing that causes this tipping point is none other than the force of discrepancy.

The implications are staggering. The chaos we experience in our heads and the emotions they generate are not what ultimately cause our emotional upset. The ultimate cause of our upset is the medicine called discrepancy. In a world rife with war and destruction, we fall under the false impression that the cause of our combined horror is war and destruction. This is an emotional, surface-level reality. In a world where opposing beliefs lead to hatred, we believe that those who believe differently are the cause of our hatred. This, too, is an emotional, surface-level reality. Underneath the surface of our emotional suffering is a hidden truth. This truth called *discrepancy* appears anytime we accept delusional beliefs of self and others as reality. We must state this message over and over again because, for many people, it is hard to believe their suffering is based on mindlessly accepting false beliefs of self and others.

It might sound simplistic but it is anything but. Discrepancy causes complex changes within our biological and psychological world that lead to the effects of dissatisfaction. As we said before, it is not the chemicals that are the fundamental cause of our emotional issues, instead discrepancy is the thing that causes the chemicals to become imbalanced in the first place. As previously stated, without a scientific understanding of this aspect of life, it is easy to say these views are misguided and wrong. It is also easy to say that ten thousand years of sacred knowledge is wrong simply because it cannot be verified to be scientifically correct. Is the sacred knowledge lacking or is our science yet to be able to understand it?

Go to www.andyschoenfeld.com for more (FREE) life-changing wisdom!

CHAPTER 13: ANOTHER LIE: WHAT WE SEE AND HEAR IN OUR HEAD IS NOT REAL, IT IS IMAGINARY

We have been told a lie that says, "What we hear and see in our mind is imaginary, and thus it is not real." This is not true. Though what we hear and see in our minds might not be true to our physical senses, it is nonetheless a reality to what we call our *inner, intuitive senses*. It is the same thing as with the proverbial silver lining within a cloud: we can say that even though we can dream of potential solutions to our problems, in the end, those solutions are simply imaginary. As previously stated, they are only imaginary to our physical senses but quite real within the world of our inner intuitive senses.

It is these latent potential solutions inherent in our lives that are discrepant with our mindlessly accepted delusions. While we mindlessly accept a voice that tells us "there is no hope," there is another message to be heard, one that we assume to be imaginary. It is the presence of these hidden potentials — potentials based on life's mandates for growth, harmony, and balance — that cause us to experience the effects of discrepancy. These potentials are the light within suffering that will allow humanity to adapt and change so as to create a more satisfying experience.

The realization that we are not consciously, or intentionally thinking, combined with the idea that what we hear and see in our imagination is real to our inner intuitive senses allows us to withstand the emotional discomfort of discrepancy. These realizations allow us to look inside our discomfort and find the treasure of wisdom within it. This treasure — the potential to awaken and the potential to create value — does not sit above our dissatisfaction. Instead, it sits right in the middle of it. Neither the treasure nor the dissatisfaction sit above or below one another, but rather they both exist simultaneously in the middle of our experience of suffering. When we try to stop, run away from, numb, or mindlessly blame ourselves or others for our emotional discomfort, we miss out on the opportunity to look within the discomfort to find the treasure.

When we identify ourselves with what we mindlessly listen to in our heads, we only solidify our identification with limitations. When we identify others by what they mindlessly say, or what we mindlessly hear in our heads regarding them, we only solidify within our minds and theirs an identification with limitation. But when we can look within our inner intuitive world and find the proverbial silver lining within the cloud, one of endless potential, we can identify ourselves with that potential. Learning how to do this is vitally important for when we learn to access our inner intuitive world we learn to experience the source of these potentials and the ultimate law that gives rise to it. The potential to create value is no different than its source, as a rose is no different than the essence that brings it into existence. There is not one way to find what I am speaking of, for there was more than one sage that has taught it. It is up to each individual to seek out their teacher who will help them discover what the following reveals.

When we identify ourselves with the ultimate law — one that awakens potential from non-existent to existent, one that gives rise to all things nonexistent and existent — then we can identify others by the same law. While we sleep, we only know of birth and fear death. But when we awaken, we can identify ourselves and others with the law that transcends both. This is the law that gives rise to both, the law by which we can rightfully identify ourselves because it is our true, fundamental essence. The ultimate law simultaneously possesses both cause and effect. Putting ourselves down or placing ourselves above others serves as a cause that activates the effect of discrepancy. While one-moment discrepancy is an effect, it is at the same time a cause that leads us to self-improvement. Meaning, it is simultaneously both a cause and effect. This simultaneity of cause and effect is an attribute of the one, single, and wondrous law.

This experience is called appreciation. The knowledge that our source — that which brings us from potential existence into physical existence — will not accept our mindless descent into delusion *is* the experience of delight. The knowledge that the fundamental law — the true aspect of who we are — can never be extinguished, even at the end of our temporary existence, is to know comfort and security. The knowledge that all forms of life, the environment, and the societies contained therein all stem from this same law is to know of respect. This is the appreciation, delight, comfort, security, and respect that is the true intention and essence of the fundamental law we speak of.

CHAPTER 14: THE INNER WORLD OF THE COLLECTIVE

You possess an imagination that is not tethered to the physical mandates of your body. This imagination or inner world does not belong to any single individual as it belongs to the collective. Within this inner realm exists everything that ever was or could be potentialized to an infinite number of possibilities. Within the inner world, life neither exists nor is non-existent, so it is free to explore all forms of constructive and deconstructive potentials. Your physical senses are bound to the laws of the physical world, for that is the way that life survives within a human body. Life in the inner realm does not have such limitations, for it realizes all potential as eternal in the ether of the inner world and temporary within the physical world.

Imagine that our world of "thinking" is as natural as our breathing. Imagine if we were to take an impartial stance, listening with an impartial attitude to what we hear in our heads. If we were to consciously accept the mind vomit, we could pay attention to the dissatisfaction at any time when delusion would appear. We could accept the imbalance with the knowledge that it is discrepant from life's mandate, and through that acceptance, we may lift the weight of delusion. Instead of fearing what we hear and feel, we could accept it with an impartial attitude. This would open up the possibility of *choice* — not "choice" as in "you" choosing, but "choice" as in hearing. This aspect of hearing would be no more complicated than the act of seeing for a man who has sight, or the act of breathing for a man of health.

The person who fears that what they listen to in their head or feel in their body will be tethered to those fears, and as a result, will mindlessly create more of it. This only reinforces and perpetuates delusion. Within that fear, they will hear the mind create concepts that are the opposite of that which they fear. Wherever there is the potential for a god, there is likewise the potential for a devil. Wherever there is the potential for discomfort, there is likewise the potential for comfort. This is how creativity works within the mind. An idea of failure will naturally create ideas of success. Mindlessly fearful of failure, a man will run in the opposite directly toward ideas of success. This is not a choice; it is a forced fantasy. It is running from one feared aspect of duality to another aspect that one assumes is safe. It is like a man who runs toward bliss, while really he is terrified of the 'ugly' within him.

When a person with calm reassurance observes and accepts the delusions that they hear in their head, then they can listen to and identify themselves with the source of that reassurance. The experience occurs effortlessly because it is not forced. This is because they are not bothered by the two extremes, for they accept both sides equally. Take, for example, the extremes of discomfort and comfort. The wise person will not prefer one over the other, for fear does not fuel them. One may achieve this state through acceptance. Through acceptance, a person will be aligned with truth, and that which they hear in their head will follow suit. What they hear will not come from the construction of delusion, but instead from a connection to the wisdom of creation. With eyes to see and ears to hear, they will no longer run from one extreme of discomfort to another extreme of comfort, for they will rest within the middle. This is the comfort of natural choice.

When a person with a neutral stance accepts unsatisfying emotions, they can look within themself. Peering inside, one can see these emotions as clearly as one remembers a dream. We all experience dreams as real as if we are experiencing them first-hand. Acceptance allows us to step outside the dream and calmly experience all of the noise, drama, and disruption that our emotions create. Once outside the dream, we realize that the experience is temporary and not a part of the physical world. Likewise, outside of the dream of a person's life, the reality of emotional dissatisfaction is understood as discrepancy. This reality may be invisible to our physical senses, which know of negation. However, this same reality is readily observable by our inner, intuitive senses that see beyond the physical realm. Therefore, this reality exists and does not exist at the same time. This reality is the treasure of the ultimate law that sits within emotion.

When humanity practices this neutral acceptance of all things, we all can perceive our entire lives as clearly as a dream, all the while without being bothered or attached to it. These are the imaginings of a clear-headed world. There will be no conflict with what our minds say, for we will be aware of it speaking. We will be neither frightened nor elated by what it says. When we collectively untie the knot of personal reality, we will "think" as effortlessly as breathing. This so-called "thinking" will be no different than seeing, breathing, tasting, or feeling, for what we hear will clearly reflect that which the law of balance says. This is the voice of logic and reason that speaks in terms of satisfaction and dissatisfaction. This is the voice of the fundamental law that brings life into existence.

Neils Bohr: "Everything we call real is made of things that cannot be regarded as real."

Einstein: "God does not play dice."

Regarding logic and reason, there is always a potential choice to be made and a potential effect to be experienced. All of this comes down to questions regarding perspective. Does an infection indicate that one is sick or that one is healing? Sickness is not personal; the body does not perceive sickness as "bad," nor does it perceive "healing" as good. Just like how healing restores the body to balance so that it once again can function efficiently, the universe also is very efficient.

CHAPTER 15: WE ARE LIVING THE WRONG NARRATIVE

No one bothered to tell us that humans are a cooperative species. It might be hard to swallow, especially if we have ever turned on the news. But it is true: we are a cooperative species, living the wrong narrative in a competitive world. It's not that humans don't like to compete, but that they only like to do it for fun. We know of the theory of evolution, which states that a species grows when it is challenged. But it's not like we are finches that have to adapt to changing conditions outside of our control. Our adaptations are not meant to pertain to our physical survival. We don't have to grow a new big toe to navigate the earth or develop wings to fly. Instead, our development is meant to be an expansion of our consciousness and awareness. This expansion of awareness will allow us to see that our lives are not limited to the bounds of our physical bodies. Our physical senses may have their limits, but our inner, intuitive senses are connected to all life forms, including the planet itself.

The term, "inner, intuitive senses," refers to the senses that we possess but are not physical. They are similar to our physical senses, except that they are thousands of times more sensitive. These senses are designed to perceive the vast potential realities that exist within the inner world. Within this inner world, life's coloring book, imagination, plays with all potentials that ever could exist. Our physical senses, tethered to our subconscious understanding of life, would not be able to process or tolerate the vastness of this experience, for it goes against the physical laws of our earthly life.

The inner world is the realm of the collective universe where life experiences infinite potential without the fear of death.

This is the playground within which all forms of life play. This is where we communicate with all other forms of life. This is where our life and all other life forms exist as one. This reality is brought into question by the simple lie which says, "that what we see in our imagination is not real." Fixated by delusion, hinged to fight, freeze, or flight, we operate only with the awareness of physical senses that cannot perceive the wonders of the inner collective world.

Imagine what it would be like to experience what others in the collective experience. Imagine what it would be like to feel their joys and their sorrows. If another person's experience was felt as our own, would we still rely upon justifications to lie, steal, hurt, or maim anyone else? If we experienced ourselves as another person, would we rely upon "do unto others as you wish they do unto you"? Or would we rely upon, "Do it to others before they get to do it to you"? If we could walk within a mother's experience of giving birth, would we ever consider killing? Within the inner world, all such potentials are experienced with the full weight of their emotion, but it is done as a potential expression of life, enacted so you can wisely choose which experiences to bring into the physical world. Unaware of the inner, intuitive senses and the inner collective world, we all end up following the mindless whims of our emotions. Asleep, we become the tiny "I," "me," or "my," which is our solitary experience. Disconnected from the collective, we are divorced from the spirit of the collective, a spirit that is based on mutual respect and consideration for all forms of life.

This disconnection only leads to disruption and dissatisfaction, the experience of discrepancy. We cannot be satisfied with life when we experience ourselves as disconnected from it. This is because our life is not limited by the bounds of our physical body, for it lives also within all the other life forms on the planet. If other life forms on the planet are suffering, then we will not find happiness — that is unless we take some kind of action to alleviate it.

If we wish to find happiness, we might want to adjust our

definition of it. Happiness is not acquiring things. Acquiring things is an achievement. Happiness is not an achievement. It is also not a "ha ha" experience like laughter or having fun. It is not something we will find within or through our bodies. This is because happiness is not something that we can possess, for it does not belong exclusively to any one individual. It lives and resides within the inner world of the collective. Within the inner world, happiness is a potential, but through practice, we can birth it into the physical world by caring for one another and the world. By cultivating the ability to hear a voice of calm assurance, a voice that is available to all of us, and learning to rise above the delusion of "I," "me," or "my," then we will experience a victory. Achievements are based on temporary phenomena, like buying a house or having a relationship. These achievements will eventually fade. But a victory, found by rising above delusion, can never be taken away, for it is etched into the book of life. Once registered, it is experienced by the collective, whether others are aware of it or not.

The same is true for suffering. Whether we are aware of it or not, we are all affected by things that take place within the collective. War, poverty, or homelessness might not be your experience, and some people might see them as inconveniences. But outside of our awareness, they are registered as suffering within the collective. This is neither a theory nor a latent potential, but rather it is an actuality. It defies logic and reason to assume that we are divorced from events and the experiences of others as we sit in front of our computer screens or T.V. monitors. Sure, we can turn off our TVs or look away, but this cannot prevent our intuitive senses from feeling, seeing, and hearing the collective world scream. With this awareness, our personal development takes on added significance. As we learn to climb above our distorted views of life, our victories become victories registered within the collective. A single life contains a billion light bulbs, but that individual life has only one switch which can turn on only one light. When we help others and teach them to find clarity, it allows us to access the billions of light switches that are within the billions of people in this world. Within the inner intuitive world, we are one body. When we rise, so does the whole body of the collective.

We can learn to become aware when we mindlessly listen to and accept delusions as reality. We can learn to pay attention to disruption as it throttles within us. When we know that it is discrepancy speaking, we acquire a clarity that allows us to accept what we experience emotionally. This clarity acts just like a bodily fever that burns out a virus. When the pain of discrepancy fades, we can look within the experience and find the silver lining within the cloud. When this happens, people will no longer live by forced mandates, as they will be able to hear the wisdom of life speak within them. This is called natural choice. We can all learn to hear this voice instead of listening to one that either puts us down or places us above others. We can learn to live within the calm assurance of this voice. When people can feel the sanctity of life come alive, they can perceive the same sanctity in others. The inner world of the collective will awaken within us, where we are not against each other, but bound by our collective connection. This is a world that can accomplish miracles. When we are seven billion strong, there is no room for defeat.

Go to www.andyschoenfeld.com for more (FREE) life-changing wisdom!

CHAPTER 16: WE ARE THE SOUND OF THE HUMAN COLLECTIVE AND THE COLLECTIVE UNIVERSE

On one hand, we are singular instruments, while on the other, we are the sound of an entire orchestra. As a single instrument, we play our part, but when combined with other instruments we become the combined sound. We are both individual instruments, while at the same time, we are the combined sound of the collective.

When we fall into delusion, we fall under the impression that we are the ones writing the music. Arrogantly, we believe that music is our vehicle for self-expression. Attempting to put emotion into music, we use our physical senses to dictate what is to be heard. The music is then forced, chaotic, and unbalanced. This is music of delusion, self-importance, and arrogance.

When an artist is free of the weight of delusion, they do not write but instead can hear the sound come from the ether and then write it down. The mixture of melody, harmony, and rhythm is heard in perfect balance. From the ether, they can hear and experience sounds that disrupt the senses, but they remain unperturbed as they write them down. From the ether, they can hear and experience sounds that are jubilant, but are not carried away as they write it down. With a clear head, they allow life to be the composer and willingly write down what life dictates to them. The joy of hearing both sounds that disrupt and sounds that lift the spirit is equal. Emotions are accepted and experienced, whether they are emotions of sadness or joy. Because they have studied, they can use established techniques to bring into the physical world sounds that come from beyond. Because they had practiced, the experience takes place effortlessly. Compared to the willing acceptance of hearing life speak, all else becomes secondary. As the world becomes still, the body will find calm — regardless of whether it plunges into music of despair or music of joy.

The experience is no different for a person who is not a musician. We all possess the ability to hear a voice coming from the depths of our lives. This is the voice of choice that we can use to write our narratives. This is the ability to realize that the distortion that is naturally created by discrepancy is designed not to hurt us but to alert us to our errors. When one is able to fully feel this distortion and accept it — bearing in mind that the discrepancy does not indicate personal deficiencies or malevolence on behalf of others — we can then maintain balance. It is then that we identify ourselves with the nature of grace as it speaks to us.

Imagine walking along a tight wire laid on solid pavement. Now imagine someone telling you that, if you are not careful, you will fall off the wire and hurt yourself. Naturally, you would remark, "Where in the world will I fall? The line is lying on the solid pavement." As such, you approach the line with calm assurance and walk along it without hesitation. But now imagine yourself five hundred feet up in the air, walking along that same tightwire. Without having mastered the art of walking on a tightwire, your only thought would be, "What happens when I fall?" Your calm assurance of safety is now gone. Imagine again being able to walk the wire suspended high in the air, but this time with the same sense of calm and assurance as when the wire extended along the solid ground. This experience is very similar to feeling calm and assured when faced with discrepancy. We must be able to walk along the wire that extends down the middle way, with the reality of truth on one side of the rope and the reality of delusion on the other.

CHAPTER 17: A NEW KIND OF DIAGNOSIS: THE DIAGNOSIS OF BEING HUMAN

Any time we mindlessly place ourselves above or below others, we experience the emotional disruption of discrepancy. Imagine if instead of simply experiencing the unpleasant emotion, we also experienced a visual distortion. Continuing to fall into our deluded beliefs about self and others, our vision blurs to the point of blindness. At this point, we naturally assume there is something wrong with our eyes.

To restore our vision, we would need to become aware of relationships. The relationship we have with the deluded voice in our head will certainly change as we let go of the idea that we are thinking. As we grow accustomed to the idea that we are listening, we learn to observe the voice in our head. In doing so, we grow aware and begin to notice those moments where we mindlessly accept falsehoods as real.

One day, emotional feelings of dread besieged a person. At that exact moment, they hear a voice in their head that says, "Nothing ever works out for me, and nothing is ever going to change." All of a sudden, they arrive at a profound, jaw-dropping realization. They say aloud, "I didn't start that conversation. It started all on its own." They still hear the noise in their head, but it now sounds as if it is coming from an adjacent room. There is now a presence of calm, a stillness that stands between them, and the mind vomit. The presence of this stillness completely wiped out the validity of delusion and in that moment of clarity, the power of the emotion just dropped away.

This is the hidden reality of peace that sits within delusion and the emotional disruptions of discrepancy. This reality is the treasure of the ultimate law that sits within suffering. This is the experience for which we should all seek. This is the "how," as in the question, "How do I discover the treasure that sits within suffering?" This is the "how" as in the question, "How can I enter into a state of calm awareness?"

This knowledge does not require mere intellectual acknowledgment. Rather, this knowledge is an ontological experience that dissolves the validity of our delusions and the emotional sensations of discrepancy that come along with it. This practice does not seek to stop unpleasant emotions or the harsh voices that we hear in our heads. Rather, it is a practice that turns on a light of awareness. Once the light is turned on, the validity or truth of what we hear in our head ultimately fades.

Our attachment to this hypnotic "dream reality" we call life separates us from the hidden, inner truth. This hypnotic dream is known to our physical senses through a voice we hear in our heads and emotions we feel in our bodies. Within this dream, the truth of the inner, intuitive world is only a whisper. But with the remembrance of a single moment of clarity, we can remember our inner intuitive world and the treasures that lie within it. This is an experience where we physically feel an emotional narrative, while simultaneously remembering another inner narrative. To transcend our physical experience, we must discern the lies of delusion and enter into the inner world. Here we become the observer, instead of the interpreter, of what our minds are saying and our bodies are emotionally feeling. When we become witnesses to the events in our minds, the validity of those events is nullified.

For any of us to make this work, we must be able to impartially observe the mind vomit from the moment it spills. It often starts with an 'I," "me," or "my" statement. Examples may include: "I can't do anything right;" "Nothing goes right for me;" or "My life sucks." Alternatively, the "I," "me," or "my" could be hidden in a statement regarding others. For example: "They don't give a crap!" Even though the phrase does not explicitly contain the word "me," it is nonetheless implied. It could also come in the form of, "What the hell is the matter with them" or "Those people don't know anything." Whether it is about "I," "me," "my," or "them," the common denominator is the emotional feeling of discrepancy that accompanies it. To make this work, we must pay attention. We are talking about untying the knot of personal reality, and since we are so accustomed to living within the hypnotic reality of emotion, it takes a great deal of practice to untie it. This is no different than an "ah-ha" experience of sudden insight, where the world seems to stop and we bathe in realization.

Through practice, we all can create such a victory where the sensation of peace replaces our painful emotions. The freedom of this experience is breathtaking. It is from this space of clarity that we begin to hear a different sort of inner voice, a voice that resonates with the mandates of life. From within this space of awareness, we can peer into the mysterious aspects of life. The questions we have about the fundamental essence of life are not simply answered; instead, the answers are experienced. The profound feeling of this space speaks to us through the language of indescribable happiness. It is like having a conversation with an essence that has neither a face nor a body, and it has neither lips nor a mouth. This fundamental essence does not need those forms, for it has *us* to speak through instead.

All products — even the awakening of consciousness described above — should come with a disclaimer, so pay attention to the following warning: just because somebody experiences this victory once does not mean that they will live in this state forever. However, it does mean that once we do experience it, we will know how to reach it again. This means that while the experience of clarity can always be lost to new spews of mind vomit, the memory of clarity will stay with you for as long as you live. The only way to return to this wondrous experience of clarity is practice.

Go to www.andyschoenfeld.com for more (FREE) life-changing wisdom!

CHAPTER 18: BEYOND DUALITY

As we practice obtaining clarity, we will naturally fall back into the delusions of wrong views of self and others. When this happens, we will listen to the delusion that says we are somehow failing. This is based on the delusion that happiness is some kind of spiritually fixed state that we can stay within once we achieve it. This delusion can be ministered through entering our inner intuitive world where happiness and misery are not experienced as two separate things. Our physical senses tell us that happiness is the opposite of sadness. But to the world of our inner intuitive senses, we can realize the oneness of happiness and suffering.

In one moment, life appears, and in the next moment, it disappears into death. As life constantly comes from nothing into something, appears and disappears, and oscillates between being and extinction, it is evident that these two cycles occur eternally. It is no different from happiness and suffering. At one moment we call it, "happiness," and then in the next, we call it "suffering." In our inner intuitive world, we realize that they are two sides of the same coin. Physical life appears and then disappears into death. Death is only life waiting to rediscover itself as physical. Happiness appears and then disappears into grief. Suffering is only happiness waiting to rediscover itself, just as death is life waiting for rebirth. This illusion continues until we finally accept both cycles as one ultimate reality.

The experience of neutral acceptance allows us to improve our relationship with logic and reason and the source of life from which it stems. Untethered from the burden of delusion and uncoupled from the weight of emotion, we can experience and identify ourselves with the essence within us. Untethered from delusion, the realities of happiness and sadness, self and others, and birth and death, all become apparent to us. Within this reality, we realize that all of life is one and that one life lives through trillions of life forms. Through clarity, neutral acceptance, and realization, we are elevated from a singularity to the collective called "us." This experience will improve the relationship we have with others and the relationship we have with the collective universe.

Go to www.andyschoenfeld.com for more (FREE) life-changing wisdom!

CHAPTER 19: THE SEVEN SECRETS OF PSYCHOTHERAPY, REVISITED

The first secret. We have been told that what we hear in our heads are our thoughts. We also have been told that if it is taking place in our head, then we are the ones thinking it. This is not true. What we hear in our head is neither intentional nor consciously driven; it is driven by our subconscious mind. This being the case, we should refrain from saying that we are "thinking," and in its place start to use the more accurate word, "listening."

The second secret. What we hear in our heads forms a hypnotic reality that we assume is real. We must ask, "Why do we unquestioningly listen to and accept the words we hear in our heads that put us down, discredit us, or place us above others? Why do we listen to hurtful words which we would never consciously ascribe ourselves to being?" The answer is that subconscious images move beyond the speed of light, and the brain turns those images into the words we hear in our heads and the emotions we feel in our bodies. Because the process moves so quickly and results in the words we hear and emotions we feel, we get mistakenly and hypnotically fooled into the idea that we are thinking. Therefore, we need to become aware that we are not thinking but rather are listening, without awareness, to the contents of our subconscious mind. To see this process at work, simply ask yourself what you ate for lunch or dinner yesterday, and "see" what happens.

The third secret. We can call this negative internal dialogue "limiting beliefs of self or others," "delusions," or simply put, "mind-vomit." Whatever we call it, it paints an incorrect view of life. We have been taught that our emotional problems stem from either the things that have happened to us in the past or unfortunate things that are taking place in our current life. This is vastly different from the idea we propose, which is that suffering stems from our mindless acceptance of limiting beliefs. Based on an understanding of the *fundamental law of life*, we say that "any time we accept limiting beliefs of self or others – beliefs that go against or are discrepant to the *mandates of life*, which are limitless growth, potential, harmony, and balance – we are designed to feel emotional disruption." The emotional disruption is the experience we call *discrepancy*. With this understanding, we can say that emotional disruptions are not indicators that there is something wrong with us. On the contrary, they prove that the wondrous, fundamental law of life is working within us to capture and direct our attention and yield positive change.

The fourth secret. We should not have to use our limiting beliefs, mind vomit, to form a diagnosis regarding anyone's emotional health. When we hear words in our heads that put us down and say that we are inferior or not good enough, we conclude that we are either depressed or have some kind of inferiority complex. Then, when we engage in our mental health systems and repeat over the mind vomit, the "professionals" arrive at a similar conclusion. Except this time, it is called a *diagnosis*. We can be diagnosed as depressed, having an anxiety disorder, or any number of various emotional disorders. Therapists, social workers, psychologists, psychiatrists, and nurse practitioners all work within our current mental health system, a system that uses client's complaints to form a diagnosis of the status of their mental health. However, this mandate is outdated. Diagnosing a client based on their subconscious mind vomit does not allow for any distinction between the clients' subconsciously-driven delusions, otherwise known as "mind vomit," and their conscious intent. Additionally, it works to solidify the clients' personal identification with their mindlessly accepted delusions.

It's like taking the most painful parts of a person and using those parts to define the individual. We should not elevate our mind vomit to the level of conscious intent and then use it to form conclusions about who or what we are. Instead, we must begin to rewrite our understanding of human suffering. We can do this by understanding the influence that our spiritual nature has on our biological and psychological well-being.

The fifth secret. There is a more direct path towards happiness. On the surface, the workings of this secret appear like pain, but there is a different reality hidden beneath this surface. Underneath, there is an inner, intuitive reality that speaks of the truth of humanity. We must look within and identify ourselves not only with this truth but with the very source of the truth, that which is called the "fundamental law of life." The fundamental law of life is the reality that gives rise to emotional suffering and personal rebirth. When we align with the fundamental law of life, we essentially step back into our true identities and the purpose for which life has designed us.

The sixth secret. When we experience our true identity, one that is no different than the law that gives rise to our lives, it will forever change how we perceive ourselves, others, and the world. Imagine what it would be like if we all could see our suffering and happiness as two parts of one dream. Imagine if we could experience our suffering as caused by the same thing that gives rise to our joy. No longer will we have to blame ourselves or others for our emotional suffering, for we will have gained the requisite clarity of mind to perceive the truth of our lives.

The seventh secret. It only takes one moment of clarity to change your entire life. We have already answered the question, "How do I go about experiencing all these wonderful things?" But the mere reading of these intellectual facts differs tremendously from the actual experience of them. The seven secrets provide you with an intellectual basis, but it is your conscious intent and consistent practice that will unlock these wonderful experiences.

One day you will be caught up in your emotional suffering. You will hear a voice in your head. That voice will either put you down, limit you in some way, or place you above others. In one moment, you will experience *discrepancy*, feeling all of the bad emotions that typically accompany the mind vomit. But then, in the blink of an eye, you will have a profound realization: *I did not start that vomit-driven conversation.* This significant moment of clarity will forever change how you experience yourself and the world around you. You will stand in awe as you hear the delusions speak, and it will feel as if you have overheard them from an adjacent room. The validity of its message and the unpleasant emotions that accompany it will vanish. In its place, you will experience a sense of self that can only be described as wondrous. The more you practice this awareness, the more clarity you will have, and likewise the more you will be able to identify with the feeling of wonderment and the source from which it springs. I promise you that if you continue to practice this way, it will forever change the way you experience yourself, others, and the world.

What would it be like if these were the experiences to which our friendly strangers would lead us? Gone would be the endless back and forth that elevates mind vomit to the level of conscious intent. Instead of trying to find happiness through exploring misery, we would have a direct path to uncover the joy of our being. We would learn *The Greatest Lie Ever Told*, *The Sacred Mother of All Rules*, and the function of discrepancy. We would not need to learn any sort of technique or read a manual. We would only need to practice elevating our awareness. There is no single technique to enact this; it requires only practice, plain and simple.

Those who practice could freely share with others their experiences opening the door to clarity. They could show others how to understand how delusion sets off a disturbance within the physical senses. They can inform others that no one should try to interpret these emotional disturbances while still emotionally preoccupied by them or the comings and goings of the physical world. Instead, they can teach others to leave their preoccupations with the physical world behind and pay attention to the inner, intuitive world. This is done by teaching people how to focus inward with their eyes closed or open. With eyes open, it is said that one should not move their eyes, but fix them on a single object until a state of daydreaming occurs. With eyes closed, one can simply pay attention to their breath until the same state is achieved. People can learn to inquire from within this state, "What is the message within this delusion that I need to hear?" Simply repeating this single sentence over and over, no matter what mind vomit arises, will bring up answers from the depths of the inner, intuitive world.

By teaching these simple things, we would help people ease their burden of discrepancy until they can find these inner messages. From this, people could realize that their suffering is not an indicator that they are broken, but an indicator of life's logic and reason speaking to them. By demonstrating a calm, neutral acceptance, we can teach them how this state is obtained. This way, they can find the treasure of logic and reason that sits within the discrepancy. People could then begin to align themselves with the voices of logic and reason, as well as with the source from which they stem. This is a reality that has existed in the world in the past, and it can be a reality that we reawaken in our present lifetime.

What if one society taught this to another, and then that society taught it to others? What if this became so commonplace that we all experience the fundamental reality of life? We would find the sanctity of life within ourselves and others and leave behind the hideous idea of war. This does not mean that we will not disagree with others. These realizations will allow us to know of ourselves as more than a human collective; they will allow us to know of ourselves as entities of the one, single, wondrous law.

Elevated beyond the delusion of the self and others, we can realize that we are not separate from nature, but that we all are a part of nature. We are the waters, the land, and the forests. We are the birds, animals, and insects. Our face is the sky and the world is our body. We are the essence that gives rise to everything. We do not pollute ourselves, for we are the waters. We do not ravage ourselves, for we are the land. We do not burn the forest, we do not harm the animals, we do not scorch the sky, and we do not destroy the world — for they are all us.

The ultimate reality of life can be seen in our bodies, our society, and our environment. As a part of this world, we know not to pollute it. As a part of the universal collective, we know to respect the collective heavens we live within. We do not detonate nuclear bombs on the planet, for we know that what we do on Earth reverberates in the heavens. We do not need to invade space with our military hardware, for we no longer need military hardware. We do not mindlessly create dangerous narratives regarding beings whom we have not met, nor do we mindlessly assume that we are the only intelligent species in the universe.

Go to www.andyschoenfeld.com for more (FREE) life-changing wisdom!

SUMMARY

Imagine what it would be like if you could become the sky, the clouds, the rain, and the space they inhabit. Imagine if you became the landscape, holding within yourself trees, flowers, plants, and all that lives within it. Imagine if you could become everything and everywhere all at once. You would be the canvas and the paint, the image and the message. You would be the one who walks and the space within which you walk. With no thought and no effort, you would become everything forever.

Before we conclude, let me tell you a story...

Go to www.andyschoenfeld.com for more (FREE) life-changing wisdom!

EPILOGUE: THE YOUNG MAN AND THE SAGE

One day, a sage came upon a young man sitting in the field, crying. The sage asked, "What's the matter?"

The young man said, "I have decided to stop trying to find happiness, but all I feel now is this ache in my stomach."

The sage said, "Isn't that the same ache that caused you to seek happiness in the first place?"

All the young man did was continue to cry.

The sage then asked the crying young man, "Do you have a foot?"

The young man stopped crying and said yes but not before asking, "Why would you ask

me such a thing?

The sage not paying attention to his question said, "So you have a foot, but do you

identify yourself as a foot?"

The young man said, "No."

Then the sage said, "You have a finger, but do you identify yourself as a finger?"

The young man once again said, "No."

The sage got down on his knee, looked the young man in the eyes, and asked, "So why, when delusion flows through your mind, why in the world do you identify yourself with it?" The sage then turned to a field of trees and asked, "Do you see those trees blowing in the wind? What would you say if I told you that I am doing that with my mind?"

The young man laughed and said, "I would say you are crazy."

Then the sage asked, "But what if I told you I can observe the trees blowing in the wind, what would you say?"

The young man said, "I would agree with you. I, too, can observe the trees blowing in the wind."

The sage stood up and inquired, "So when the vomit of delusion blows in your mind, why do you mindlessly identify yourself with it instead of simply observing it?"

The young man heard the words of the sage, but it did not stop him from continuing to complain about his suffering. He went on and on about how hard his life was and how he was burdened by his problems.

The sage smiled and asked, "Why are you paying so much attention to your delusion? If you continue to do so, you will never come to understand that it is all mindlessly spewed vomit. You will then identify yourself by this 'mind vomit' and say things like, 'I am miserable' or 'I am inferior.' Just because there is vomit does not mean that it is an indicator of anything other than the presence of the vomit."

As the sage walked away from the young man, he stopped, turned around, and said, "When you take a crap, do you call yourself a crappy person?"

The young man stood up and laughed. He said, "No, why do you ask?"

The sage turned and began to walk away when he pointed to his head and said, "So when this craps, why do you make such a big deal about it?"

A few days later, the sage came upon the young man once again. The sage, seeing that the young man was still upset, asked "What is the matter?" The young man started to go through a long list of personal problems when the sage interrupted him. "Tell me, what did you have for dinner last night?"

The young man, surprised by the question, answered, "I start telling you of my suffering and you want to know what I had for yesterday's dinner?"

The sage didn't bat an eye and said, "Yes."

The young man said, "What does yesterday's dinner have to do with anything?"

The sage didn't budge. "Well, what did you have?"

Exasperated, the young man raised his head and moved his eyes around. The sage interrupted the young man's moment of reflection and asked, "What are you doing with your eyes?"

The young man said, "Give me a moment, I'm thinking."

The sage tried to say something, but within a few seconds, the young man snorted and said, "Beets and potatoes."

The sage smiled and said, "I love beets," and began to walk away.

The young man, still upset, yelled, "I'm glad that you love beets, but what did your question have to do with my problems?"

The sage turned around and said, "When I asked you what you had for dinner, did you hear the words beets and potatoes, or did you see a picture?"

The young man walked up to the sage and said, "I saw a picture, but what does that have to do with anything?"

The sage said, "Everything." He then pointed to his head and said, "It tells you how this works. All I did was ask you a question, which you then asked yourself. Then you started moving your eyes around. What did you say you were doing?"

The young man said, "Well, I was thinking."

The sage said, "Maybe that's what you call it, but to me, you were looking for something. Once you found it, you heard the words beets and potatoes. Now to you, it's called thinking. But to me, it's more a matter of searching, seeing a picture, and then listening as the picture is turned into words." He continued, "It was no different when you were complaining about your problems, except when you complained, you might not have been aware of any pictures. But that does not mean they are not there. They are simply out of your awareness."

The young man, still exasperated, said, "What in the world does this have anything to do with the problems I was trying to tell you about?"

The sage said, "It tells you that when you complain, you are not consciously or intentionally doing anything aside from parroting the noise that you hear in your head." And then the sage asked, "Are you intentionally sitting around and trying to feel miserable, or does all the misery just pop up in your head?"

The young man pondered for a second and said, "Well, it just comes up by itself."

The sage proclaimed, "Time for lesson one. When the sudden noise in your head either puts you down or places you above others, it is called 'mind vomit' or 'delusion.' Or we might call it 'false views of self and others.'" He continued, "Lesson two. You are not intentionally doing it. Lesson three. Since it happens beyond the speed of light and is accompanied by pictures and words that you hear in your head and emotions that you feel in your body, you are under the impression you are thinking." The sage elaborated, "Then, you begin to identify yourself by this experience and come to whatever conclusion the noise in your head is dictating to you." The sage concluded, "When you mindlessly fall into the 'mind vomit' that spews in your head, you form what is called a discrepant self-identification."

The young man asked, "What do you mean 'discrepant?' Don't you mean negative, miserable or unhappy?"

The sage, now walking away, turned back and said, "That lesson will be for another day."

Days passed before the young man saw the sage again. When the sage approached him, the young man said that he was still very upset and plagued by what he referred to as "the demons in his head."

The sage laughed and said, "I see you're still playing with your vomit."

The young man took offense at the sage laughing at him. "This is not mind vomit! My problems are real."

The sage took a step back and said, "Okay. For now, your problems are real, and not vomit. But let me ask you, do you find lasting satisfaction within your suffering?"

The young man said, "Nobody finds lasting satisfaction in suffering."

The sage replied, "Actually, that is not the truth. But if that is the case for you, then tell me... What is the cause of your dissatisfaction when your demons appear?"

Not understanding what the sage had just revealed to him, the young man said, "I just don't like the way it feels."

The sage replied, "No one likes the way sadness or anger feels, but what *causes* your dissatisfaction?"

The young man said, "Are you asking what causes the suffering or what causes me to not like it?"

The sage saw that the young man was getting confused, so he said, "Let's just say you don't know the answer."

The young man sighed and said, "You are right, I do not know."

The sage said, "Maybe it causes you such upset because you're identifying yourself by your delusion. You know, it's impossible to never feel bad. But it just might be possible that you can get to the place where feeling bad is an indicator of something good inside of you."

The sage sat down on a large rock and told the young man a story:

Once upon a time, a great sage thought to himself, *How can I cause my disciples to find the ultimate joy?* After pondering it for a while, he came upon an answer.

He entered a nearby town and found where the young children gathered to play. He waited until nighttime, and once everybody was asleep, he took the most precious of jewels and placed them just underneath the dirt. He knew that it would rain that night and that as a result, the dirt would turn to mud, fully concealing the precious jewels.

The sage sat by the side of the road and waited until the morning when the children could come out to play. Whenever the children would begin to walk towards the mud, their mothers would yell at them. "Stay away from the mud! We know you want to make mud pies, but the mud is dirty and defiled."

The sage knew the nature of children, that as soon as their mothers looked away, they would sit in the mud to make mud pies. To make the best mudpies, the children would have to sift through the mud so that they could pull out any small rocks. Only pure mud could make the *best* mud pies. The sage watched the children as they dug their hands deep into the mud, slowly pulling out first one rock and then another. When they lifted the muddied stones out of the ground, the children noticed that certain stones were smooth and perfectly rounded. They went quickly over to a nearby puddle and washed the rocks. Before long, they realized that they were not rocks, but precious jewels. They ran back to their mothers, exclaiming, "You said that mud was defiled, but look what we have found!"

Intrigued by the story, the young man asked, "What did the mothers say to their children?"

The sage said, "They were astonished, but they didn't believe the children. They said, 'We don't believe that you found such jewels in filthy mud.' Of course, that didn't stop them from taking the jewels from the children. As for the children, from that day forward, they gleefully waited for the rains to come so they could look within the mud for more hidden treasure."

The young man looked at the sage and asked, "If the great sage had such riches, why would he make children sift through mud to find it?"

The sage stood up from his seat and said, "Joy in life is not getting things; it is found in discovering them. Each time you look within the mud or *delusion* within your life, you can discover treasures beyond your wildest dreams."

The young man and the sage began to walk back to their village. As they were walking, the sage said, "When you see the world through your delusions, you look upon the world through the eyes of delusion. Thus, what you see are illusions. But this does not stop the essence of your life from doing its job. Life will not allow you to mindlessly accept a limiting self-identification without trying to get your attention through feelings of dissatisfaction. That feeling of dissatisfaction is called *discrepancy*; it is the energetic distance between your deluded ideas of yourself and your true essence. The feelings of dissatisfaction within the experience cause you to seek knowledge." The sage continued, "When you earnestly seek knowledge and wisdom, the potential for wisdom becomes manifest. That's when you begin to see the world through the lens of this wisdom." "But if you try to run from the dissatisfaction," the sage warned, "then you will never find the wisdom within your delusions."

The young man then asked, "Then how do I find the wisdom within my

dissatisfaction?"

The sage smiled and said once again, "That is a lesson for another day."

The young man woke up from his sleep, turned to his wife, and said, "Today I will go back to the edge of town and speak to the sage because I have some questions for him."

His wife said, "What sage are you talking about?"

A strange look came upon the young man's face. "What do you mean, what sage? The sage that I told you about, the sage that I met yesterday."

His wife looked at him and said, "You were with your mother yesterday; you didn't meet with any sage."

The young man jumped out of bed and rubbed his head. Confused, he stammered, "But I distinctly remember meeting with this sage."

His wife laughed and said, "Maybe you had one of your vivid dreams'."

The young man protested and said, "No, it was not a dream, I remember it very clearly."

"If you are so certain that you met with a sage, what did he say to you?"

He paused and tried to think. He searched his memory but could not remember what they had talked about. As the night's sleep left and the reality of the day took hold, he remembered that he, in fact, was at his mother's house the previous day. He turned to his wife and said, "But it all seemed so real. I don't remember anything that the sage said, but I have this incredible feeling inside of me like my spirit was given the gift of flight. I might not remember what was said, but to the world of my spirit, it is all quite as real as the nose on my face." And then, as if a candle came alive by the strike of a flame, he said, "And it was not just one meeting, it was multiple times that we met together."

The young man couldn't shake the feeling that he had met with a sage, but as the days passed, he began to realize that it was a meeting that took place only within his dreams. But as hard as he tried, he could not remember what they spoke about. He began to berate himself for not remembering such an important encounter. In time, his search to remember what the sage had told him led him into great despair. Within this despair were feelings of frustration that told him that he would never find what he was looking for. Also within his frustration were feelings of anger that told him he was incapable of ever finding out what the sage said. Behind that anger was a terrible fear that he would spend the rest of his life suffering. Deep within all of these feelings was a profound sense of sadness that he had carelessly missed an opportunity to find the solutions to his problems.

Days turned into weeks, and weeks into months. The memory of the sage faded into a preoccupation with life's troubles. He found himself right back in the same miserable condition he was in when he first encountered the sage. Feeding his family, taking care of his mother, and making sure his wife and children had a home in which to live consumed his every waking moment. He began to argue with his wife and scold his little children. Outwardly he would blame his wife for not taking care of the house or the children, while silently and inwardly he blamed himself for not being able to provide them with a better life. He would fight with his neighbors, while he silently thought that they all saw him as a failure.

Unable to manage this despair, he found his only escape in sleep. As soon as his wretched day would end, he would crawl into bed. But in time, this too became another ordeal to live through. His once peaceful sleep became filled with nightmares. He began to toss and turn on a nightly basis. He would cry and scream so much that his wife made him sleep outside with the horses in the barn. After a whole night where he experienced tormenting nightmares, he would wake up still exhausted.

A year passed. At this point, he felt that there was no

difference to him between being asleep and awake. By night, he would experience nightmares. By day, he would experience the very same nightmares. The only difference was that in the daytime, he would experience nightmares with his eyes wide.

One night, the young man had a particularly violent nightmare. He dreamed that he had lost his home and that he was forced to live with his family in the streets. Standing in the rain, listening to his children and wife cry, he looked up into the dark sky and screamed, "What else could happen to us? What other misfortune can come our way?"

Then, all of a sudden, within the sky, images began to appear. Hundreds, thousands, millions of images, each one a complete story unto itself. Anything and everything, an infinite amount of scenarios that could go wrong, that could bring him pain, appeared before him. There were scenes of sickness, poverty, and death. There were scenes of grief, sadness, and unbearable fear. He looked up to a sky filled with images of suffering and cried, "Is this all life has to offer?" Then everything went black.

Everything that was there a second ago vanished into complete darkness. Standing within this total darkness, he heard a voice begin to speak. He didn't know who was talking to him, but it seemed very familiar.

"Life is infinitely creative. It takes a single event and exhausts every infinite potential that could exist. The two cycles of creation — construction and deconstruction, existence and nonexistence, birth and death — are infinitely played out. Events begin and end, and potentials unfold in all directions, and all at once. Thus, the two cycles occur simultaneously. To you, there is a single event with a single memory to remember it by. But to the world of your inner senses, a single memory is potentialized into billions of potential memories. You are only aware of the memories that you can digest with your physical senses. But to your inner senses, these potential memories are as real as the five fingers that are attached to your hand. Within a single memory of pain, there are potential memories that tell another story where solutions are found and where joy is experienced. When you are filled with mindless fear, the result of delusion, you are not able to go within to experience these potential memories. This is because, within delusion, you cannot see that you are mindlessly accepting limiting views of self and the world. But when you understand that you are not the one consciously doing it, a doorway opens. When you understand that you are not the one thinking, you instantly become the one who can observe what is being said. When you understand what you hear comes from your subconscious mind, clarity is achieved. This is the path to the clarity of a single moment. This is where you align yourself with the inner, intuitive senses that realize the potential of everything and anything that ever was or could ever be. This is where you rise above yourself and become everything."

It took only a moment for the young man to do as the sage instructed. He realized that his suffering was not of his conscious intent. The clarity of that one, singular moment burned away delusions the way a fever burns out a sickness. As he rose above his singular identity, he perceived, free of delusion, the emotions that once plagued him. Inside these emotions, he found endless treasures of wisdom. Upon hearing this wisdom, he realized its source. He joined with this source, and right before his eyes, a single image from within his heart left his body and was projected onto the sky. As he looked up, all he could see was his own face smiling down upon him. Words spoke from within him, "The sky is your face and this world is your body." It was as if time had stopped. He no longer saw through his physical eyes, but instead observed everything taken in by the eyes within his mind. He no longer heard through his physical ears, but instead experienced all the sounds captured by the inner sense of hearing. His will to breathe was replaced by the breath's gentle gift of rising and falling. His suffering ended as his heart, all on its own, broke open for him to experience its boundless treasures. Within his smiling face, he perceived images that brought him endless delight. He saw his family as safe and happy, he saw himself within a community of welcoming neighbors, and he saw his children grow and prosper.

The voice stepped out from the shadow and formed the image of the sage. He said, "Within you are treasures, but not with your physical senses will you perceive them. Remember the most sacred of all teachings that you have just now experienced, a teaching that produces clarity and wisdom. In one moment, you have realized the eternity of that moment. You have experienced the wonder of clarity as you have observed your mind speaks all on its own. The fire of this clarity has wiped clean all of the delusions that gave rise to anger, sadness, guilt, frustration, and fear. You embody the very experience of boundless joy. You have risen above who you think you are, and you have become what you are, the essence of all life. Finding this treasure takes but a moment, but that one moment will last for your entire lifetime."

The young man rose from his bed, put on his clothes, and walked out of the door of his barn. As he walked down the road, he came upon a man yelling at his neighbor. All of a sudden, the young man woke up. The voice in his head said, *this man has fallen into his delusion and is now spewing it out of his mouth. He is under the impression that he is thinking, but in reality, he is only listening to his delusion come alive in his head.*

The young man continued to walk down the road. He came upon a mother fussing with her child. The mother screamed, "Why do you have to make me scream for you to hear me? I said stay away from the mud." The voice in his head said, *this woman too has fallen under the influence of her delusion. Within that delusion is the idea that it is her child that causes her discontent; thus, she believes that her child is the one making her feel frustrated.*

The young man continued further down the road. He came upon an old man crying on the side of the road. He asked the old man why he was crying. The man said, "I am old, I cannot do the things that used to come so easily to me. I am weak and no longer useful to this world." The voice in the young man's head spoke once more. *This man too is not conscious; he is mindlessly accepting his delusion and identifying himself by it; thus, he sees himself as useless.*

The young man continued down the road. He came upon a young woman whose sadness hung from her face. He asked her why she looked so sad. She said, "All I feel is a deep sadness. No matter what I do, I cannot lift its veil." Weeping, she continued, "I don't know what is wrong with me." Once more the voice spoke in the young man's head, saying *you must ask if there is something wrong with her, or is there something right within her that will not allow her to find satisfaction in her delusion. Like the old man you just met, she is identifying herself with the delusion she hears in her head. Under its influence, she is unaware that her dissatisfaction is not within being sad but instead, her dissatisfaction stems from her mindlessly driven beliefs about it.*

The young man practiced for years. He practiced the art of being aware. He practiced the way of observing what he heard in his mind. He practiced accepting the distortion of discrepancy. He learned to cultivate the ability to hear delusion through a clarity that allowed emotion to no longer be a concern but instead, a teacher bringing him the joy of wisdom. He continued to practice joining with and identifying himself with this clarity, as he was able to identify himself with the essence that gives rise to it. The young man learned of these ways and practiced them until he grew into an old man.

Many years later, while walking through his village, the old man came upon a young boy sitting in a field crying. The old man asked, "What's the matter?"
The young boy said, "I have decided to stop trying to find happiness, but all I feel now is this ache in my stomach."
The old man said, "Isn't that the same ache that caused you to seek happiness in the first place?"
The young boy said, "The only thing I know of is that it hurts."
The old man said, "Tell me what you believe is the cause of your ache."
The young boy told him a story about breaking his mother's favorite jar, how she screamed at him, and how he now believes that he is a bad little boy.

The old man said, "Sonny, one thing I have discovered is that within all problems is a silver lining. Even within your most unpleasant emotions, you can find wisdom. But you have to learn to look for it. Everything that I will teach you, I learned from a great sage. At times he spoke to me in person. At other times he spoke to me in dreams. Some other times he spoke to me as a voice in my head. Be it in person, in my dreams, or within my head, he taught me everything I now know."

For the next few years, the old man visited with the young boy every week. He would patiently listen as the young boy spoke about the difficulties in his life. His mother was poor, his father had died, and his brother constantly got into trouble; more times than not there was not enough food to eat. For years he listened and then taught the young boy what he had acquired. He taught him that most of the time he is not consciously thinking, but instead *listening* to the voice in his head. He taught the boy about the nature of delusion or what he called vomit. He would say, "If it either puts you down or places you above others you must question its validity." He told the young boy that if he fell into his vomit then he would identify himself by it. He taught him about discrepancy and how its medicine is called dissatisfaction. He taught him that this dissatisfaction is the best part of him trying to get him to see the best within him. He taught him the sacred teachings that bring clarity and wisdom, the wonder of clarity in observing the mind speak all on its own. He told him that the fire of this clarity would wipe clean all delusions that give rise to anger, sadness, guilt, frustration, and fear. He taught him that when this happens, he would be able to look within those emotions and find their hidden treasures. He taught him that through this experience, he would identify his life with the essence that gives rise to life. He told the young boy that he would become an experience of boundless joy. He told him that when this happens, he will rise above who he *thinks* he is and become *what* he is, the essence that is all of life.

As weeks turned into months and months turned into years, the young boy finally grew into a young man. One day he complained to the old man about the difficulty of coping with his emotions. He said, "As much as you have taught me, there are still times when I have a hard time seeing the value hidden in my pain." The old man, having grown wise in his years, handed the young man a very large, rough, and ragged piece of wood. He told the young man that the wood, while very rough, was wood from a very special tree. He said, "When you are struggling with the distortion that comes with discrepancy, I want you to take this rough piece of wood and begin to sand it down. Don't try to sand the entire piece, just work on one tiny section at a time. While you sand it, you must ask yourself, 'What is the message of wisdom within this emotion?' You are to continue to do this until you find wisdom within each: anger, sadness, frustration, guilt, and fear. When you have found the wisdom within each, come and see me."

And so the young man did as the old man instructed. When he fell into anger, he would reach for the wood and sandpaper. When he would fall into sadness, frustration, guilt, and fear, he would do the same. The young man practiced this just as the old man had instructed. He practiced these ways for three years until he found what he was instructed to find. By the time he had come to see the wisdom within all of his emotions, he realized what the old man was teaching him. He held in his hand what was once a distorted, rough piece of wood, now refined into the most precious of objects. *It wasn't about refining the wood,* he thought, *it was about refining my mind so I could find the treasure that is within my life.*

Finally, after years of searching within himself, he went to tell the old man what he had discovered. To his dismay, when he reached the old man's home, he discovered that he had died. Waves of emotion passed through his body, but he remained unperturbed, for he had discovered the wisdom within suffering. He felt so indebted to his teacher that he went home, took the treasured piece of wood, and brought it to the old man's grave.

He placed the wooden treasure by the grave and said, "I have felt emotion to the extent that I can hear messages of wisdom within them. Anger is wanting more of yourself, to give more, to be more, to reach for the highest for yourself and others. Sadness is the difficulty of accepting a condition or situation. Frustration is knowing better but not choosing. Guilt is a misuse of our ability to reflect and change so that we do not repeat the same mistakes. And fear is falling so far into delusion that all potential is completely unseen."

He stood by the side of his teacher's grave and said, "At this moment I have no anger since I have given myself fully to what you had asked. I have no sadness, for I accept the cycle of life that has brought you to the other side of it. I have no frustration because I have chosen my task wisely. I have no guilt because I have corrected my misdeeds of falling into my emotions. And I have no fear, for I have risen above the world of suffering and happiness and aligned myself with the law that gives rise to both."

As years passed, the young boy grew into a man, and years more passed until he too had grown into an old man. He practiced the ways of his teacher until he acquired so much wisdom that the townspeople began to call him a sage.
One day, the sage was walking through the village when he came upon a young man. He felt that there was something very familiar about him, but he couldn't exactly place what it was. The sage asked the young man, "What's the matter?"
The young man said, "I have decided to stop trying to find happiness, but now all I feel is this ache in my stomach."
The sage said, "Isn't that the same ache that caused you to seek happiness in the first place?"
The young man asked, "What do you mean?"
The sage, now recognizing who the young man was, asked, "Do you not remember?"

The young man said, "Remember what?"

The sage replied, "Do you not remember who you were the last time we did this?"

The young man pondered and pondered until his eyes lit up. His face glowed and his body bent over in laughter. He looked at the sage and said, "I remember, I remember it all."

With eyes as bright as the sun the young man said, "The same thing that caused us to be reborn is the same thing that causes our physical death. Death is life waiting to rediscover itself once again as physical life. Over and over it cycles. Disappearance into nothing, extinction into being. What causes it, creates it. Constantly coming from nothing into something, appearing and disappearing. Life appears to rediscover itself, and physical life ends so the discovery can happen again. It is no different with happiness and suffering. Happiness appears and disappears into suffering. While they appear as two separate things, they are at the same time one thing. One will continue to seek happiness as an alternative to suffering until one accepts both cycles as one reality."

The sage looked at the young boy and remarked, "In our last life, I was the young boy and you were the sage."

The young boy said, "And before that, I was the young boy and you were the sage."

The sage laughed and said, "And in the one before that, I was the boy and you were the sage."

Both of them were now beside themselves with laughter. Through tears of joy, they both said at the exact same time, "The universe has a really big sense of humor."

THE END.

THE SEVEN SECRETS OF PSYCHOTHERAPY

Heard and written down by Andrew Schoenfeld, Circa 2024

Go to www.andyschoenfeld.com for more (FREE) life-changing wisdom!

ABOUT THE AUTHOR

Andrew R. Schoenfeld, LCSW is a licensed clinical social worker who runs a private practice in Shelton, CT. He is the author of *The Seven Secrets Of Psychotherapy*, *Tales From Candyland*, and the composer of the jazz opera *The Moon of Eyderean*. In addition, he worked as the producer for the Mike Longo DVD series *The Rhythmic Nature of Jazz*.

A practicing Nichiren Buddhist of forty years, Andrew sought to explain in practical English the psychological implications of the last teachings of the historical Buddha, *The Lotus Sutra*. Andrew's mission is to teach others the life-changing psychological and spiritual insights he gained from over forty years of practice as a clinical social worker, musician, and writer.

www.ingramcontent.com/pod-product-compliance
Lightning Source LLC
Chambersburg PA
CBHW071925020426
42331CB00010B/2728